PREFACE

It is hoped that this latest edition of THE BOOK OF THE J.A.P. will assist the many owners of J.A.P. engines to obtain maximum trouble-free running at minimum expense. It deals with four-stroke J.A.P. engines and accessories from 1927 to 1952 or, in other words, practically all J.A.P.'s now in use on the road.
During 1949-50 two J.A.P. two-stroke engines of 98 c.c. and 125 c.c. were introduced, also a new 1100 c.c. Mark 1 racing engine. J.A.P. two-stroke engines are *not* covered in this edition, and it should be noted that full maintenance instructions are not included in respect of every type of racing and speedway engine. In the majority of cases, however, the racing engines do not vary from the standard type engines except in regard to the lightening of certain parts and the use of higher compression ratios.
A description of the S.V. vertical twin J.A.P. engine, and some reliable maintenance instructions have been compiled with the kind assistance of the J.A.P. drawing office (see Chapter IV).
Chapters V, VI, and VII contain instructions for owners of A.J.W. and Cotton motor-cycles dating from 1934 onwards. The 1952 single-cylinder Cottons show little change in design, but the 1939 single-cylinder A.J.W. "Flying Fox" has been discontinued and was replaced in 1948 by the "Grey Fox" with vertical twin engine. It is dealt with in Chapter VI.
It should be noted that the book applies not only to motor-cycles referred to in Chapter VIII, but also to earlier makes of machines such as the Brough Superior, Montgomery, O.K. Supreme, Federation, etc. In addition the book may be of service to owners of J.A.P. engined three-wheelers, small trucks, lawn mowers, etc.
It is worth recalling that J.A.P. engines have been in continuous production for about forty years and that in April 1937 a J.A.P.

PREFACE

engined Brough Superior smashed the world's record for a flying kilometre at the creditable speed of 169·8 m.p.h.

Thanks are due to Messrs. J. A. Prestwich & Co., Ltd., for assistance in the preparation of the book, and also *The Motor Cycle* and *Motor Cycling* for kindly permitting some excellent engine drawings to be reproduced.

W. C. HAYCRAFT

FLOYD CLYMER'S MOTORCYCLIST'S LIBRARY

The Book of the
J.A.P.

PRACTICAL MAINTENANCE OF FOUR-STROKE J.A.P. ENGINES (1927 ONWARDS). DEALS WITH 1934-52 A.J.W. AND COTTON MOTOR-CYCLES. CHAPTERS ON 500 c.c. S.V. VERTICAL TWIN J.A.P. ENGINE AND THE A.J.W. "GREY FOX"

BY

W. C. HAYCRAFT, F.R.S.A.

ANNOUNCEMENT

By special arrangement with the original publishers of this book, Sir Isaac Pitman & Son, Ltd., of London, England, we have secured the exclusive publishing rights for this book, as well as all others in THE MOTORCYCLIST'S LIBRARY.

Included in THE MOTORCYCLIST'S LIBRARY are complete instruction manuals covering the care and operation of respective motorcycles and engines; valuable data on speed tuning, and thrilling accounts of motorcycle race events. See listing of available titles elsewhere in this edition.

We consider it a privilege to be able to offer so many fine titles to our customers.

FLOYD CLYMER
Publisher of Books Pertaining to Automobiles and Motorcycles

2125 W. PICO ST.　　　　　　　　　　LOS ANGELES 6, CALIF.

INTRODUCTION

Welcome to the world of digital publishing ~ the book you now hold in your hand, while unchanged from the original edition, was printed using the latest state of the art digital technology. The advent of print-on-demand has forever changed the publishing process, never has information been so accessible and it is our hope that this book serves your informational needs for years to come. If this is your first exposure to digital publishing, we hope that you are pleased with the results. Many more titles of interest to the classic automobile and motorcycle enthusiast, collector and restorer are available via our website at www.VelocePress.com. We hope that you find this title as interesting as we do.

NOTE FROM THE PUBLISHER

The information presented is true and complete to the best of our knowledge. All recommendations are made without any guarantees on the part of the author or the publisher, who also disclaim all liability incurred with the use of this information.

TRADEMARKS

We recognize that some words, model names and designations, for example, mentioned herein are the property of the trademark holder. We use them for identification purposes only. This is not an official publication.

INFORMATION ON THE USE OF THIS PUBLICATION

This manual is an invaluable resource for the classic motorcycle enthusiast and a "must have" for owners interested in performing their own maintenance. However, in today's information age we are constantly subject to changes in common practice, new technology, availability of improved materials and increased awareness of chemical toxicity. As such, it is advised that the user consult with an experienced professional prior to undertaking any procedure described herein. While every care has been taken to ensure correctness of information, it is obviously not possible to guarantee complete freedom from errors or omissions or to accept liability arising from such errors or omissions. Therefore, any individual that uses the information contained within, or elects to perform or participate in do-it-yourself repairs or modifications acknowledges that there is a risk factor involved and that the publisher or its associates cannot be held responsible for personal injury or property damage resulting from the use of the information or the outcome of such procedures.

WARNING!

One final word of advice, this publication is intended to be used as a reference guide, and when in doubt the reader should consult with a qualified technician.

CONTENTS

CHAP.   PAGE

I. ENGINE LUBRICATION 1
II. DECARBONIZING AND VALVE GRINDING . 14
III. ADJUSTMENTS AND OVERHAUL . . . 33
IV. THE S.V. VERTICAL TWIN J.A.P. . . . 65
V. HINTS FOR 1934-9 A.J.W. OWNERS . . . 77
VI. CARE OF A.J.W. "GREY FOX" (1948 ON) . 88
VII. HINTS FOR COTTON OWNERS (1934 ON) . 107
VIII. J.A.P. ENGINED MOTOR-CYCLES . . . 130
     APPENDIX 135
     INDEX 144

CHAPTER I

ENGINE LUBRICATION

THERE is a close analogy between the heart of a man and the oil pump of a petrol engine. Both are responsible for circulating a supply of vital fluid throughout all the working parts, and the moment that supply weakens, serious trouble results. For 494 c.c. S.V. vertical twin engine, see pages 66-8.

Five Golden Rules. To ensure a J.A.P. engine being correctly lubricated it is extremely important to observe five rules, which are as follows—

(1) Always use a recommended engine oil (see below).
(2) Always maintain sufficient oil in circulation.
(3) Keep the oil clean.
(4) Prevent the oil becoming diluted.
(5) Do not forget to run-in the engine carefully during the first 800-1000 miles (see also page 69).

Suitable Oils for J.A.P. Engines. If you would get the utmost performance and life from your J.A.P. engine, you should regularly replenish the oil tank with one of the following oils recommended by the makers—

(1) Castrol XXL (XL during winter).
(2) Shell X-100 SAE 50 (X-100 SAE 40 during winter).
(3) Mobiloil BB (Mobiloil A during winter).
(4) Price's Energol SAE 40 (SAE 30 during winter).
(5) Essolube 50 (Essolube 30 during winter).

For racing purposes Castrol R is excellent, but it should be particularly noted that this is a vegetable oil and must *not* be mixed with any of the five mineral base oils mentioned above. During the running-in period of 800-1000 miles it is beneficial to a J.A.P. engine to add Acheson's Colloidal Graphite to the engine oil in the proportions of one pint to one gallon of oil.

THE DRY SUMP SYSTEM

The popularity of this system is due to its simplicity, its automatic working with the minimum of attention, and to the fact that it helps to keep the oil cool, which is very desirable. The system was first used on J.A.P. engines in 1932. A double-acting

Pilgrim pump was fitted to engines of that year, but all subsequent engines have a double-acting pump of J.A.P. design, details of which are shown in Fig. 1.

How the Oil Circulates. Oil is gravity fed from the oil tank to the delivery side of the pump which forces it under pressure to the roller big-end bearing through a drilled timing side mainshaft and crankpin drilled to correspond with the oil-way in the timing side flywheel. On some engines, however, the oil is not forced

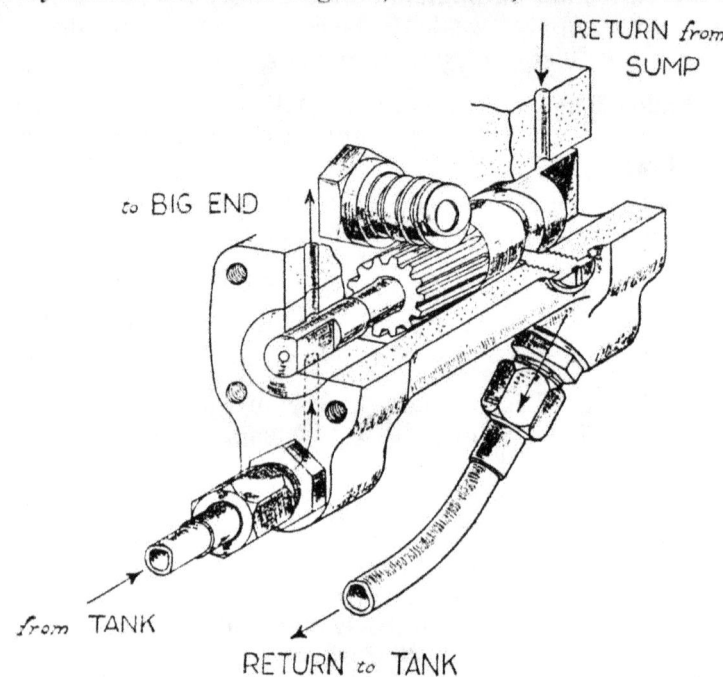

FIG. 1. THE "HEART" OF THE J.A.P. DRY SUMP SYSTEM
During 1932 a double-acting Pilgrim pump (Fig. 2) was used, but on subsequent engines a J.A.P. Mark III oil pump (as above) has been fitted

through a drilled crankpin, but breaks the surface of the inside of the flywheel boss directly opposite the big-end bearing. Oil exuding from the big-end bearing on to the flywheels splash lubricates the piston and cylinder walls. On 1100 c.c. S.V. engines an additional oil supply is fed direct from the pump to the base of the front cylinder.

The driving and timing side mainshaft bearings are lubricated by oil collecting upon the crankcase walls and draining through channels to pockets connected by holes with the bearings. Some of the oil in the crankcase is automatically conveyed into an oil-box, a special feature of most J.A.P. engines, via non-return disk valves or a rotary valve (described on page 4), and this oil is utilized on many engines to lubricate the overhead-valve gear (where fitted) or the timing side bearing. Surplus oil is returned to the crankcase.

All surplus oil in the crankcase is trapped by a flywheel scraper cast across the bottom of the crankcase and is diverted to the sump which is connected by drilled crankcase passages with the return side of the pump. The pump then returns the oil under

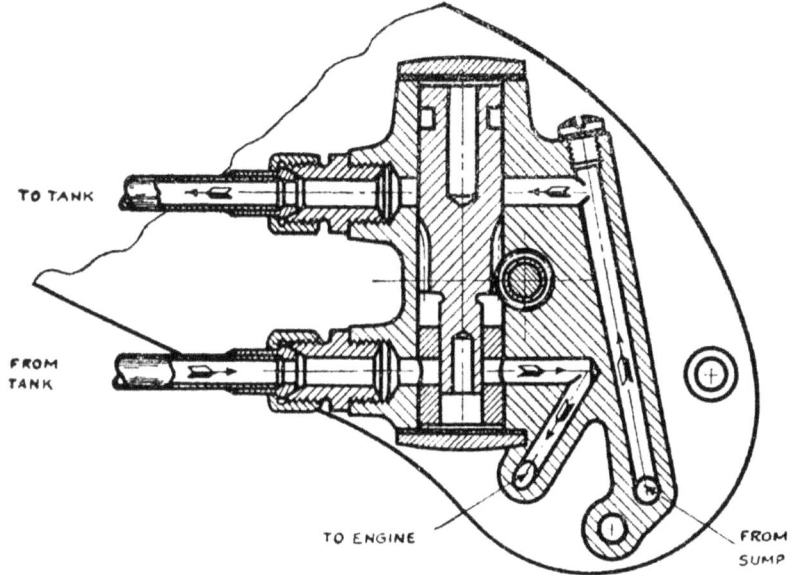

FIG. 2. SECTIONAL VIEW OF 1932 PILGRIM PUMP

pressure to the oil tank, which has a large filter to remove impurities collected during circulation which goes on so long as the engine is running. It should be noted that the return side of the pump is of greater capacity than the delivery side, so that the sump is always kept "dry." No adjustment for the pump is provided, the oil supply being automatically increased with increase in engine revolutions. See also page 8.

The J.A.P. Oil-box and Rotary Valve. As already mentioned, most engines incorporate a special oil-box for separating oil from the crankcase vapour and using it for auxiliary lubrication. On J.A.P. engines the crankcase and timing case are in communication with each other, so that oil is thrown liberally over the timing gears. It then, on earlier engines, passes into the oil-box via a set of vacuum valves and is maintained at atmospheric pressure by means of a projecting relief pipe. On many later type engines (dry sump or mechanical pump) a rotary valve (Fig. 2A) is provided. Between the timing case and oil-box there is a vertical passage which is closed at the upper end by a horizontal sleeve. The sleeve is driven off the engine camwheel at engine speed and the driven end is blanked off. The other end is in communication with the crankcase and, when a slot in the sleeve registers with the vertical passage, the descending piston forces oil mist through

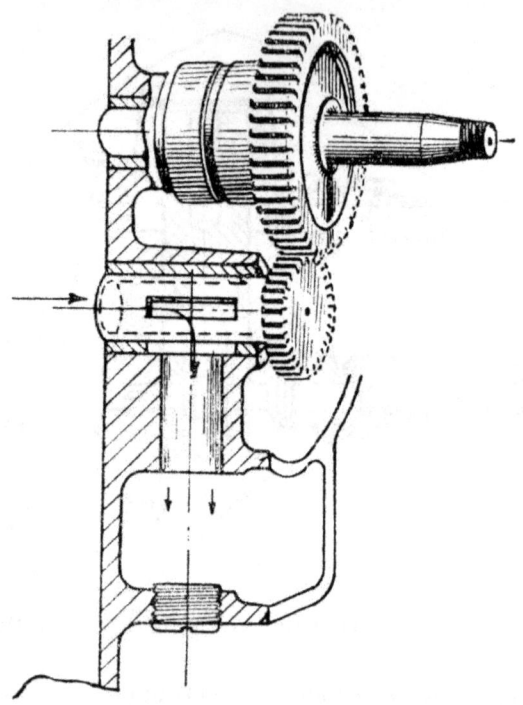

FIG. 2A. HOW OIL FROM THE CRANKCASE IS ADMITTED INTO THE OIL-BOX BY A ROTARY VALVE

into the oil-box, where it condenses, the air escaping to the atmosphere via the relief pipe and the oil settling to the bottom of the box. The timing of the rotary valve is such that the slot begins to open 65 degrees before the piston reaches bottom dead centre. The rotary valve on twin-cylinder engines should be timed on the *front* cylinder. To ensure correct replacement the rotary valve and camshaft gears are marked.

On some engines the crankcase pressure release valve has been incorporated in the timing spindle and its method of working is the same as the rotary valve just described. Correct timing is such that the leading edge of the spindle hole meets the leading edge of the bush hole 65 degrees before bottom dead centre. If at any time the off-side mainshaft is separated from its flywheel, it is necessary to mark the position of the spindle relative to the flywheels before removal.

Lubrication of Overhead Valve Gear. During 1927 grease-gun lubrication was provided for the rocker spindle bearings on O.H.V. engines, but from 1928 onwards automatic lubrication has been used. On engines designed before 1933 the bearings for the rockers were lubricated by oil mist passing up the push-rod cover tubes from the timing box. On later engines, however, the rocker-box bearings and valve guides are positively lubricated by oil drawn up from the oil-box.

Passing from the oil-box through the timing gear is an oil pipe which is connected to the rear of the rocker-box. Now the timing gear is in a partial vacuum during upward piston strokes and, since the rocker-box communicates with the timing case by means of the push-rod covers, a semi-vacuum is also created in the rocker-box, with the result that oil is drawn up from the oil-box where it is stored at atmospheric pressure. On entering the rocker-box some of the oil is trapped by webs and passed on to the rocker bearings; the remainder passes along two small pipes and lubricates the valve guides.

In the case of some O.H.V. engines including the Vee Twins and the later "high camshaft" engines (see page 8) oil is by-passed direct to the rocker bearings from the pump, the surplus afterwards returning to the sump through the push-rod covers.

Five Maintenance Points. To ensure a J.A.P. engine with dry sump lubrication working smoothly and efficiently, there are five important points which must always be looked to. Here they are—

(1) Always replenish with suitable engine oil.
(2) Keep the oil-level in the tank correct.
(3) Check the oil circulation frequently.
(4) Clean the oil tank and filter regularly.
(5) See that all pipe unions are kept airtight.

(1) Engine Oil Replenishment. The question of what engine oil to use has already been discussed on page 1, and you are advised to run on one of the five oils mentioned.

(2) Maintain the Correct Oil-level. With dry sump lubrication the whole of the oil in both the tank and engine is in constant circulation and for this reason it is exceedingly important to keep the oil-level correct. Unless this is done the oil will not keep cool and is prone to become contaminated and diluted during circulation to a dangerous extent, with the consequent risk of injuring the engine. To be on the safe side, it is desirable always to keep the oil tank *at least half full*, about three-quarters full for preference. But avoid over-filling the tank so that the level rises to more than 1 in. below the return pipe orifice, and on no account allow the level to fall below the half-full mark. The filler cap should be removed about every 150 miles, the level inspected, and the tank topped up with fresh oil if necessary.

(3) **Verifying Oil Circulation.** To ascertain that the oil is circulating properly, remove the tank filler cap and observe whether oil is being steadily returned from the orifice of the return pipe. It should issue in a regular succession of drops or bubbles. On starting up, however, it is not unusual for the flow to be erratic and excessive. Air leaks are suggested by a "frothy" return of oil, and if such is present the pipe unions should be tested for tightness. Possible causes of an irregular return are—

(1) Insufficient oil in the tank.
(2) A dirty tank filter.
(3) Choked or leaky oil pipes.
(4) A defective oil pump.

With the Pilgrim double-acting pump it is not possible to observe the oil being delivered to the engine at the pump. A tight-feed window is not provided.

(4) **Cleaning Oil Tank and Filter.** The oil tank and filter (on some machines the filter is incorporated in the tank union) should both be thoroughly cleaned on completing the running-in period and subsequently at intervals of about 1000–1500 miles. The tank should then be replenished to the correct level with fresh oil. This is most important. However carefully a machine is handled, carbon particles, metallic dust, and unburnt fuel slowly but surely contaminate the oil, and unless removed, the impurities may not only damage the engine bearing surfaces but also give rise to choked oil-ways, which is a serious matter. It is best to drain the oil tank after a run when the oil is warm and thinned down somewhat. Place a good-sized receptacle below the drain plug to catch the oil as it runs out on removing the plug and be sure that the whole of the oil is drained off. Afterwards the tank should be removed and very thoroughly cleaned with petrol, and the same applies to the filter.

If the filter is made of fabric, handle it with great care and brush it gently. Where a gauze filter is used (such as on the A.J.W. and Cotton) avoid cleaning it with a fluffy rag which is liable to choke the mesh. It is desirable to renew a fabric filter about every 5000 miles as its filtering qualities deteriorate. Having cleaned the tank and filter and replenished the former with plenty of fresh oil, prime the delivery pipe by securing the upper union and allowing oil to begin to run out before securing the lower union;

this prevents the possibility of an air lock forming. It is advisable to flush out the crankcase with flushing oil when decarbonizing.

(5) **Preventing Air Leaks.** A dry sump lubrication system will not function perfectly if there are any air leaks on the delivery or return side of the pump and therefore the unions at both ends of the pipes must be kept done up absolutely tight. It is a good plan to test the union nuts with a spanner occasionally as vibration sometimes causes them to work loose. Air leaks on the return side often cause the plug to oil up.

Oil Leakages. It sometimes happens that an engine begins to become smothered with oil on the outside, thus spoiling its appearance, preventing the proper dissipation of heat, and increasing oil consumption. Possible causes of oil leakage include the following —

(1) A choke in the return pipe or return side of the pump.
(2) A faulty rotary valve or non-return valve.
(3) Defective push-rod or rocker-box cover joints.
(4) A loose union on the rocker-box feed pipe.
(5) Leaky pump, pipe, or oil-box cover joints.
(6) Imperfect crankcase or timing case joints.

The remedies for the above troubles are fairly obvious. In the event of a choke in the return side of the lubrication system occurring, there is a strong probability of oil being forced out at some joint. Evidence of a choke would be failure of oil to issue from the return pipe, but this might also be due to other reasons (see page 6). Defective timing case or oil-box non-return valves would tend to build up pressure in the crankcase and so cause oil leakage at the "point of least resistance." Trouble with the non-return valves, however, is unlikely and it is inadvisable to remove the securing screws which in most cases are burred over on the inside. In the case of the rotary valve there is nothing to go wrong and failure here can only be due to incorrect timing of the valve (see page 4). Should oil leakage occur at the push-rod cover joints, inspect the rubber washers and, if perished or damaged, renew them. Also see that the springs at the foot of the push-rods are properly located and keeping the push-rods tight against the washers. Jointing compound should be used for the timing case, magneto chain case, and for the crankcase joints, but paper washers (oiled) should be used for the timing and magneto chain case joints on "high camshaft" engines. The oil-box has a fibre washer and the pump has a rubber ring to exclude oil. No cylinder-base washer is provided.

Pump Troubles. The plunger type of pump used on J.A.P. engines has no ball valves or delicate parts likely to need adjustment or give trouble, and a defect in the pump is a rare occurrence.

All moving parts are well lubricated and wear takes place very gradually indeed. It is imperative, however, always to keep the set-pin which projects into the cam groove right home and to see that all washers are in perfect condition. All pump joints and plug screws must be kept airtight and the use of a liquid packing such as "Hermitocoll" is advised for all plug screw threads.

When dismantling the pump for cleaning (only necessary at long intervals) be sure to remove the set-pin before attempting to remove the plunger and on no account use any force on the latter. The plunger should be pushed out from the small end after removing the set-pin and end plates. The driving worm need not be taken off as the small end of the plunger just clears it. When replacing the plunger, see that the plunger gear engages the worm on the engine pinion lock-nut and that the set-pin is located properly before screwing it fully home which should be done without any force. The J.A.P. pump body is cast in one with the timing cover and the pump plunger is readily accessible on removing the cover and end plates.

Dry Sump System on "High Camshaft" Engines. On more recently introduced "high camshaft" engines the method of oil circulation is considerably different from the system used on Standard engines and described on page 2.

To ensure thorough lubrication, the oil pump situated in the timing case cover draws oil from the tank and pressure feeds it direct to the big-end bearing and camshaft. Oil from the camshaft is caught in a trough and conveyed to a recess in a boss on the timing side flywheel. Centrifugal force then causes it to be fed to the big-end and supplement the pressure feed. The by-pass from the pump leads direct to a rotary valve in the flywheels communicating with the big-end bearing and there are thus two separate feeds to the big-end—one by gravity and the other by pressure.

As on the other engines, the cylinder walls are splash lubricated from the big-end. Surplus oil drains to the sump and is returned to the oil tank by the pump. Thus plenty of cool oil is fed to the engine so long as the tank is kept well replenished (page 5). With regard to the overhead valve gear, the valve rockers and springs are totally enclosed and lubricated by oil from the oil-box. Surplus oil drains to the crankcase through the push-rod cover tube.

THE WET SUMP SYSTEM

The wet sump lubrication system, which is a "one way" type, has the advantages that the crankcase can frequently be drained off without much loss of oil and that the oil supplied to the engine

J.A.P. ENGINE LUBRICATION

can be adjusted by means of a regulator situated on the mechanical pump.

Several types of mechanical pumps have been fitted to J.A.P. engines, namely the Pilgrim, the "Best," and the J.A.P. The Pilgrim and "Best" designs have been most widely used. These two pumps, which are mostly of the sight-feed pattern, are very similar in construction and method of working.

Oil Circulation. On leaving the mechanical pump the oil is pressure fed direct to the big-end bearing, the cylinder and piston being splash lubricated. On some wet sump engines, however, oil is fed into the timing case and flows along a groove through the timing side bearing into a circular recess in the timing side flywheel. A hole is drilled in the flywheel between the recess and the crankpin hole and centrifugal force carries the oil via this hole to the big-end. Both mainshaft bearings are lubricated by oil collecting on the crankcase and walls and draining into pockets leading to the bearings; the timing gear is oiled through the crankcase and timing case being in communication with each other, and the overhead valve gear (where provided) is lubricated from the oil-box (see page 5), or from the timing box on earlier engines.

Six Maintenance Points. The owner of a J.A.P. engine with wet sump lubrication should, besides seeing that the correct engine oil (page 1) is used, observe the following important maintenance points—

(1) Always keep the oil-level in the tank above the filter.
(2) Frequently check the oil circulation at the sight-feed.
(3) See that the mechanical pump is correctly adjusted.
(4) Keep the delivery pipe unions and sight-feed airtight.
(5) Clean the tank filter occasionally.
(6) Periodically drain and flush out the crankcase.

Level of Oil in Tank not Important. Provided that the oil-level is such as to keep the filter completely submerged, it is immaterial how much oil there is in the tank with a wet sump lubrication system. If the filter is not completely submerged, there is a considerable chance of air being drawn in and fed to the pump, thus upsetting proper circulation. In connexion with sight-feed pumps there is one point worth noting: should you replenish the tank with Castrol R (for racing purposes), it is desirable with the assistance of a little petrol or benzole to scrape the enamel off the well of the sight-feed chamber, because this vegetable oil attacks it.

To Adjust Pilgrim Pump. The Pilgrim mechanical pump is simply adjusted by turning the milled regulator disk on the left-hand side of the pump clockwise or anti-clockwise, according to whether it is desired to reduce or increase the oil supply respectively. Once the correct setting has been arrived at, it is best to leave the regulator alone. It is not necessary to turn the regulator right off each time the engine is stopped because, when the pump plunger is stationary, no oil can find its way through to the engine.

Where a new engine is concerned, it is a good plan to adjust the pump in the following manner. Get the engine gently ticking over and then temporarily cut the oil supply right off by turning the regulator clockwise as far as it will go. Then rotate it anti-clockwise until oil is observed just beginning to issue from the beak. Now further turn the regulator 3-4 of the 7 numbered divisions. This should give approximately the right setting for running-in, but if the engine "smokes" much, reduce the oil supply slowly by means of the notches between each division, whose individual "clicks" can be heard. About $1\frac{1}{2}$ turns from the full "off" position (or 25-30 drops per minute) should prove a satisfactory average adjustment for single-cylinder engines, though, as already stated, the rider should exercise some discretion in the matter. A slight blue haze should be visible at the exhaust on opening the throttle suddenly in neutral. If very high average speeds are indulged in or arduous hill climbing is undertaken, the oil supply should be increased accordingly.

To Adjust the "Best" Pump. A somewhat different form of adjustment is provided on the "Best" mechanical pump. After loosening the two regulator fixing screws, the regulator may be turned clockwise to increase the oil supply or anti-clockwise to reduce it. Positive (+) and minus (−) signs indicate in which direction the regulator should be turned. It should be noted that the supply of oil delivered by the pump is roughly proportional to the regulator position, and since for normal purposes it is desirable to set the pump to deliver about one-quarter of its maximum, it follows that the regulator should be turned about one-quarter on, the final adjustment being arrived at by noting the sight-feed, exhaust, etc. On no account attempt to adjust the regulator without first loosening the two small screws, and after making an adjustment be absolutely sure that the screws are firmly re-tightened. Neglect to do this may cause damage to the pump plunger and will in any case spoil the adjustment. As in the case of the Pilgrim pump, it is quite unnecessary to turn the regulator off when leaving the engine stationary.

How to Prime the "Best." Occasionally, after dismantling a "Best" pump some difficulty is experienced in getting the pump working properly again after reassembling it. In this case the remedy is to prime the cam block and plunger with oil and exclude all air. To do this, turn the regulator mid-way between the

" + " and " - " signs, leave the upper screw loose (two or three turns), and run the engine until oil begins to creep between the plate and pump body. Before priming the pump see that the pipe from the tank is full of oil.

What to Do if the Sight-feed Fills Up. Occasional filling up of the sight-feed in cold weather may be due merely to the viscous state of the oil, and the remedy is to increase the supply of oil for a short time, when the trouble will probably cure itself.

In the event of any small particle of dirt or foreign matter lodging between the ball valve and its seat on a Pilgrim pump, the sight-feed will fill up with oil when standing, and the ball valve should be attended to. This ball valve is situated in the body of the pump underneath the beak and the ball, spring, valve seat and passages should be thoroughly cleaned. To do this it is necessary to unscrew the glass window and then with a pair of flat-nosed pliers remove the spout or beak which is a tight push fit in the body of the pump.

Chronic and regular filling up of the sight-feed under all conditions of temperature and oil may be due to wear of the end cam or cam groove in the case of a Pilgrim or "Best" pump respectively, and the remedy is obvious; fit a new part.

Some Possible Causes of Irregular Pump Action. Trouble seldom occurs with a mechanical pump, but if oil is passed irregularly or the supply of oil falls off at high speed, look to the following three points —

(a) Examine and if necessary clean the filter in the tank or tank union. See that the level of oil in the tank is not so low as to prevent the filter being completely immersed, otherwise air instead of oil may be passed to the pump and engine.

(b) See that there are no particles of fluff or dirt obstructing the action of the ball valve or any of the passages. For remedy, see paragraph relating to filling up of the sight-feed chamber.

(c) Check that there are no air leaks on the inlet side of the pump and that all pipe unions are tight. Test them with a spanner but do not be "ham fisted."

Dismantling Pilgrim Pump. This is rarely necessary but if you must take it to bits, first and foremost unscrew the worm driving spindle bush screws and remove the worm and spindle. Until this has been done you must on no account remove or attempt to remove the plunger. The penalty is expensive damage! It should also be noted that it is dangerous to remove the worm with either the end plate or the end cam previously removed from the body of the pump. After removing the worm, remove the end plate and withdraw the plunger. When reassembling first fit the end cam (if this has been removed) and then the plunger should be inserted cam first, so that the two cams are in contact with each other. Then replace the return spring in the open end of the plunger (i.e. the end with the longest hole) and box it in with the end plate. It now remains to complete assembly by inserting the worm and screwing down the spindle bush.

Cleaning Tank Filter. On J.A.P. engined machines with wet sump lubrication a gauze filter is incorporated in the tank or tank union, and it is advisable to remove this for cleaning with petrol about every 5000-7000 miles. Although contamination of the oil by the engine does not occur, impurities of one kind or another do gradually collect on the filter and must be removed periodically, otherwise a diminished oil supply may be caused.

Flush Out Crankcase Every 2500-3000 Miles. On all wet sump engines the oil in the crankcase gradually gets contaminated and diluted, and the drain plug at the base of the crankcase should be removed about every 2500-3000 miles and all oil and sludge drained off. Do this when decarbonizing and preferably after a run when the oil is warm. After draining off the old oil, turn the oil pump regulator right off and then flush out the crankcase with one of the special flushing oils marketed by most accessory dealers. Again drain the crankcase and, if the cylinder has been removed, pour some clean oil over the flywheels before refitting it; this is advised because the mechanical pump cannot be relied upon to deliver a large supply of oil immediately, even with the regulator turned full on.

Dealing with Oil Leakage. If the engine becomes dirty on the outside through oil leakage, look carefully for one of the possible causes mentioned on page 7, with the exception of No. 1.

Lubrication of Overhead-valve Gear. The notes concerning rocker spindle and valve guide lubrication given on page 5 are applicable to engines with the dry or wet sump systems.

THE MAGNETO AND DYNAMO

Magneto Chain Lubrication. Lubrication of the magneto, Magdynamo, Magdyno, or dynamo (coil ignition) chain is entirely automatic via a ball valve or the outer camshaft bearing.

Lubrication of Lucas Dynamo. As in the case of the Lucas "Magdyno," the bearings are packed with grease on assembly and no attention is necessary until a very big mileage has been covered, when the instrument should be returned to the makers. About every 5000 miles put a few drops of thin oil into the commutator end bracket lubricator (see Fig. 3), where fitted.

Magneto Lubrication. Deal with as described for the magneto portion of the Lucas "Magdyno."

Miller Magdynamo and Dynamo Lubrication. On assembly, all bearing housings are packed with grease, and under normal conditions this should suffice for 10,000-12,000 miles. At the end

J.A.P. ENGINE LUBRICATION

of this mileage the instrument should be returned to the makers or one of their agents in order to have the bearings repacked with HMP grease. On Miller dynamos where provision for lubrication is included, insert 2-3 drops of oil about every 1000-2000 miles through the lubricator. Grease the contact-breaker (DHI dynamo) cam shaft lightly about every 500 miles. On other Miller dynamos and "Dyno-mags" smear cam lightly with petroleum jelly.

"Magdyno" Lubrication. Both the armature bearings and the gears between the magneto armature and dynamo are

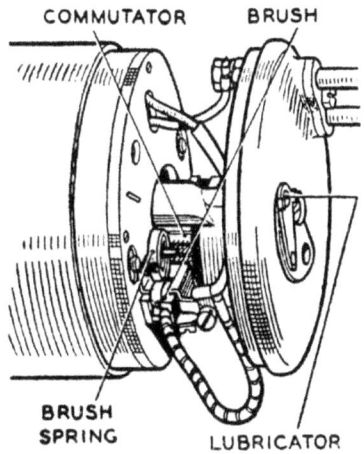

FIG. 3. COMMUTATOR END OF LUCAS "MAGDYNO" OR DYNAMO

packed with grease by the makers during assembly, and no further attention is required until at least 10,000 miles have been covered, at which time the complete instrument should be returned to the makers for cleaning and regreasing. A tip deserving of mention (applicable to Lucas ring cam contact-breakers) is to smear the rocker arm bearing with some petroleum jelly about every 5000 miles. To do this, push aside the locating spring and prise the rocker arm off its pivot. *See no lubricant gets on the contacts.*

In the case of a Lucas "Magdyno" with ring type cam, the ring cam should be withdrawn about every 3000 miles and a few drops of thin machine oil put on the felt. On a "Magdyno" with a face type cam, the wick should also be similarly lubricated. To gain access to the wick, remove the spring arm which carries the moving contact and withdraw the screw which carries the wick. It is important to see that the small backing spring is correctly replaced when refitting the arm (see Fig. 28).

CHAPTER II

DECARBONIZING AND VALVE GRINDING

IT is advisable, in order to preserve engine flexibility, high performance, and sweet running, to decarbonize singles and Vee-twins once every 2000-2500 miles (a new engine, after the first 1000-1500 miles). For S.V. vertical twin engine, see pages 70-3.

Preliminary Stripping Down. Before starting on the job of dismantling the engine for decarbonizing it is always a good plan to clean the exterior thoroughly with rags and paraffin if the engine is dirty. This facilitates dismantling and prevents the possibility of dirt getting inside the engine.

On many motor-cycles, especially those of the side-valve type, it is quite unnecessary to disturb the tank, but on some overhead-valve machines where there is not much clearance between the rocker-box and tank its removal undoubtedly facilitates dismantling and in certain instances may be actually necessary. If the tank is removed, take care not to lose the small insulating rubbers. Proceed to remove those items which hinder dismantling proper. Unscrew the sparking plug, disconnect the petrol pipe, and take off the carburettor. On most overhead-valve J.A.P. engines of recent manufacture the carburettor has a flange fixing, but some side-valve engines employ a clip fixing. On some twin-cylinder engines the induction pipe has tapered collars with nuts (R.H. threads) bored to a corresponding taper, and the pipe (Fig. 68) must, of course, be removed. Next disconnect the exhaust pipe(s) at the cylinder head and also the exhaust valve lifter wire at the rocker-box on "high camshaft" engines. On side-valve engines remove the valve caps (where fitted). As the various parts are removed, wipe them clean and lay them on a clean sheet of paper or in a box ready for reassembly. Now turn the engine over until both valves are fully closed. See also page 32.

Removing Valve Caps. On side-valve engines having aluminium valve caps it is preferable to remove the caps after allowing the engine to cool down, because aluminium contracts to a greater extent than does cast-iron. Unscrew the valve caps with the cylinder in position, as this enables good leverage to be obtained without risk of damaging the cylinder base. If cast-iron valve caps are provided, removal is usually facilitated by first warming up the engine. Examine the valve cap washers closely and, if they appear damaged or leaky, renew them, otherwise some loss of compression may occur. A good method of testing for leaky valve caps is to smear some oil around the joints and watch for bubbles on kicking the engine over.

To Dismantle Side-valve Engines. Many J.A.P. side-valve engines made in 1927 onwards have the cylinder head and barrel

FIG. 4. SHOWING CYLINDER, CYLINDER HEAD, AND ROCKER-BOX ASSEMBLY ON J.A.P. 500 C.C. SPORTS ENGINE (1938 ON)

Note the neat method of enclosing the valve springs with quickly detachable covers, the oil feed to the back of the rocker-box, and the two pipes leading to the valve guides

cast integral and it is necessary, in order to decarbonize, to remove the cylinder (see page 20) after first removing the carburettor, plug, etc. On Vee type twin-cylinder engines, deal with each cylinder separately and be most careful not to mix up any of the parts. Some side-valve engines have detachable cylinder heads with the valves situated below the head, and, unless it is desired to remove the piston in order to clean the inside and the ring grooves, the only dismantling needed is to remove the head after unscrewing the fixing bolts, which should be done in a diagonal order to prevent straining the head. If the head will not lift off readily, tap it gently upwards with a hammer applied above the inlet or exhaust port, but be sure to interpose a piece of wood to prevent damaging the brittle fins. Turning the engine over compression with the plug in position will often suffice to break a stiff joint. Handle the copper gasket with care and, if there are any signs of "blowing," re-anneal it or fit a new one before reassembly.

To Dismantle Overhead-valve Engines (Standard Type). Constructionally the Standard and Sports engines are similar, and the following instructions apply to O.H.V. engines except 1939-52 500/600 c.c. and "high camshaft" type. All O.H.V. engines have a detachable cylinder head but, before this is removed, the rocker assembly and push-rods must be taken off. On 1927-8 engines an open type rocker gear is fitted, but all 1929 engines onwards have the enclosed rocker-box type. (See also pages 19 and 32.)

On 1927-8 engines first remove the push-rods by levering open the valves and then remove the split pin on the rocker spindle and unscrew the fixing nut. The rocker spindle can now be unscrewed from the rocker standard by inserting a screwdriver in the slot provided. On no account attempt to drive out the spindle or a broken rocker standard will result. After removing the inlet and exhaust rockers the cylinder-head bolts can be unscrewed by means of the special angle-spanner provided.

To remove the rocker-box on later engines proceed as follows. Take off the rocker-box end plate by unscrewing the lever nut and then with a screwdriver or similar tool lever upwards (using the centre stud of the rocker-box as a fulcrum) each steel rocker-arm as shown in Fig. 5 until its cupped adjuster screw disengages the loose ball in the cupped end of the duralumin push-rod. This enables the push-rod and also its cover tube to be pulled right out after pressing the cover downward with the flat side of a screwdriver. Deal with each push-rod in this manner and be careful with the large oil-sealing washers inside the lower push-rod cover supports and the small washers provided at the upper spigots on recent engines.

In the case of engines made in 1934 onwards, disconnect the oil pipe at the back of the rocker-box by unscrewing the union and disconnect the two small pipes leading to the valve guides (Fig. 4). Where quickly-detachable valve spring covers are fitted, these must also come off. Now unscrew the two bolts which secure the rocker-box to the cylinder-head bolts at the front and lift the rocker-box off the cylinder head as illustrated in Fig. 6. The four cylinder-head bolts may then be removed (unscrew them diagonally) and the head gently lifted off the cylinder barrel. If

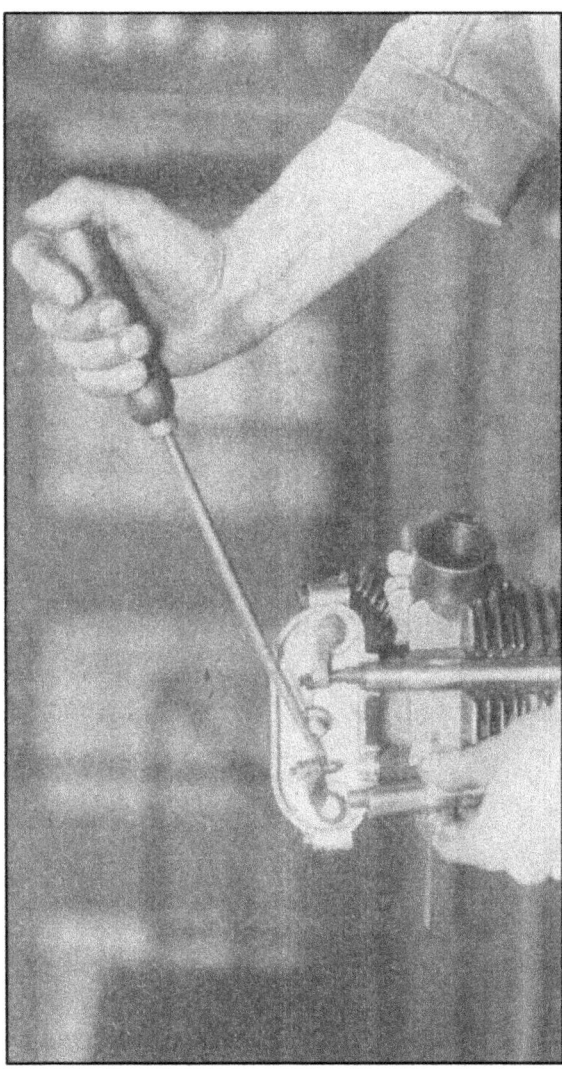

(*By courtesy of George Newnes, Ltd.*)

FIG. 5. REMOVING THE PUSH-RODS

The valve springs may be readily compressed by levering up the rocker-arms in the manner shown. This frees the push-rods which may be withdrawn with their cover tubes

the joint is stiff, tap the head gently as mentioned in a previous paragraph (page 16) on S V. engines, and do not omit to scrutinize the condition of the plain copper gasket. On some J.A.P. O.H.V.

(By courtesy of George Newnes, Ltd.)
Fig. 6. Taking the Rocker-box off the Cylinder Head

engines it is not easy to remove the cylinder-head bolts with an ordinary straight spanner and in such cases a special angle spanner (Fig. 7) is provided in the tool-kit. Having removed the cylinder head, place it in a safe place ready for decarbonizing, and if you desire to remove the piston, take off the cylinder barrel as described below. Do not do this at every decarbonizing.

To Dismantle " High Camshaft " Engines. First of all unscrew the large nut at the base of the push-rod cover tube. Then

(*By courtesy of George Newnes, Ltd.*)
FIG. 7. REMOVING CYLINDER-HEAD BOLTS WITH SPECIAL ANGLE SPANNER

unscrew the four bolts which secure both the rocker-box and cylinder head (these are integral) and remove the two together as well as the push-rod cover. If it is desired to detach the rocker-box cover from the cylinder head, unscrew the seven retaining bolts. The cylinder barrel may now be easily removed by following the directions given on the next page.

Removing the Cylinder. It is a simple matter to remove the cylinder or cylinder barrel as the case may be. On "high camshaft" engines slacken off the two top crankcase bolts as well as the four bolts securing the cylinder and head, or on other engines undo the four nuts holding the cylinder flange to the crankcase, being careful to loosen them diagonally. Before removing the nuts, however, turn the engine over until the piston is near bottom dead centre, keeping it in position by putting the machine in gear. Now grip the cylinder firmly in both hands and gently withdraw it from the piston. Where the engine is inclined in the motor-cycle frame, it is necessary to draw the cylinder off at an angle, but in many cases it is possible to lift the cylinder off vertically. No cylinder-base washer is provided. Special care should be taken while removing the cylinder not to allow the piston skirt to fall sharply against the connecting-rod or crankcase studs, and a rag should always be wrapped around the bottom of the piston. This not only prevents the risk of the piston being distorted but also prevents any foreign bodies getting into the crankcase, an accident which may cause an immense amount of bother. It is also most important when removing the cylinder not to exert any side strain which is apt to bend the connecting-rod.

On the special O.H.V. racing engines the cylinder head and barrel are secured to the crankcase by flanged bolts which screw into the cylinder head.

Piston Removal. After removing the cylinder head and/or the cylinder, next proceed to remove the piston from the connecting-rod by taking out the gudgeon-pin. In the case of aluminium alloy pistons made up to the year 1928, fully floating gudgeon-pins are used, the pin being free to move in both the small-end and piston bosses. It is important that the ends of the hard gudgeon-pin never come into contact with the cylinder walls, otherwise scoring is likely to occur, and to prevent this 1927-8 fully-floating gudgeon-pins are provided with soft end caps. Such gudgeon-pins can be tapped out from one side and the piston taken off. It is necessary, however, on the later engines to support the piston and connecting-rod firmly or else to warm the piston before attempting to remove the gudgeon-pin. This can be done by holding a blow-lamp near after removing the tank. If by any chance stiff, tap it out gently with a piece of hardwood or a soft-nosed drift interposed. After removing the gudgeon-pin a slight nick should be made on one end so as to ensure its correct replacement which is most important.

On 1929 and subsequent engines, the hollow gudgeon-pin is retained by means of two spring circlips, which bed down into grooves machined at each outer end of the gudgeon-pin hole in the piston boss. It is only necessary to remove one of the circlips in order to push out the gudgeon-pin, and this may be done by closing the ends together with a pair of small round-nosed pliers. As a rule it is advisable to renew a circlip after removal because if its springiness is affected it may come adrift and cause irreparable damage to the cylinder.

Mark the Piston. A piston laps out the cylinder in which it reciprocates in a certain manner depending upon piston thrust, lubrication and other factors, and it is most inadvisable to replace it in any except its original position on the connecting-rod; that

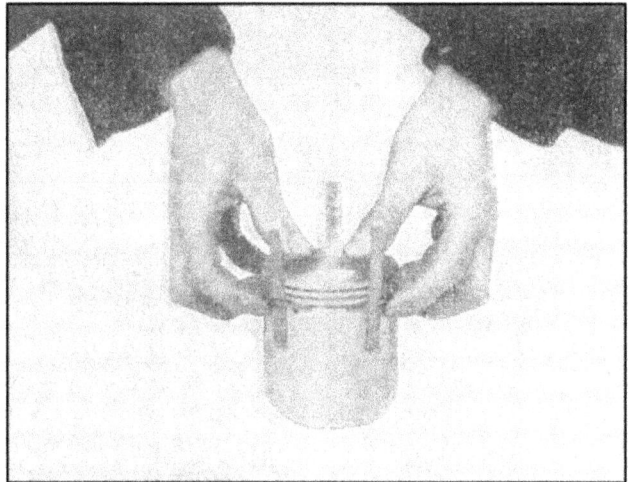

FIG. 8. A SAFE METHOD OF REMOVING PISTON RINGS
This method (see text) besides eliminating the risk of breakage is also least calculated to damage the lands between the rings or the piston ring grooves. Use the same method for refitting rings

is to say, it should not be replaced back to front or vice versa. Therefore, unless the piston has some distinguishing characteristic it is always advisable to mark it to ensure its correct replacement. Perhaps the best plan is to scratch an " F " on the inside to indicate which is the front. Be careful not to interchange the pistons on a twin-cylinder engine, and always remember that a piston should be handled with care as it is readily distorted or cracked.

To Remove Piston Rings. Piston rings being made of cast-iron are very brittle, and it is generally unsafe to open the rings and slip them straight off by hand owing to the considerable risk of breaking them which may cause much inconvenience if spare rings suitable for the particular engine concerned (and no other rings will do) are not at hand. Piston rings should never be sprung out wider than the diameter of the piston, and the best and safest method of removing the rings is illustrated in Fig. 8. Three strips of sheet tin (about 20 gauge), approximately 1½ in. long and ⅜ in. wide, are inserted under each ring, starting at the upper ring and keeping the strips evenly spaced. Each ring can then be gently slid off. Broken pieces of an old hacksaw blade answer the same purpose, but if this method is used be careful not to let the teeth touch the piston. Also be very careful with the ring grooves as aluminium alloy is very easily chipped or scratched. Where a scraper ring is fitted on the piston skirt make a note as

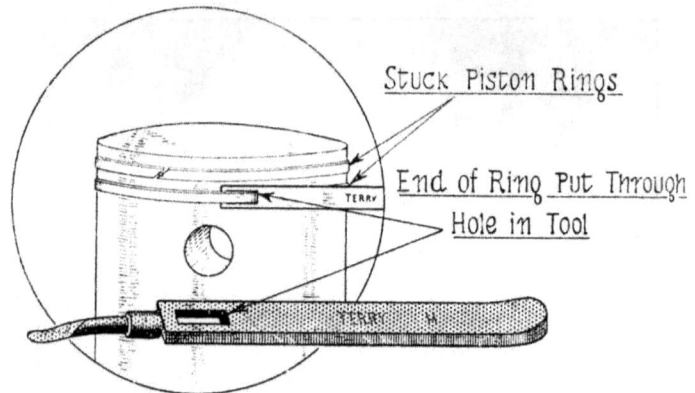

FIG. 9. A HANDY TOOL FOR REMOVING STUCK PISTON RINGS
This worth-while tool is obtainable from accessory firms, and removes stuck rings most effectively

to exactly how it is fitted to ensure its being replaced with the scraping edge the correct way up.

Stuck Piston Rings. Considerable difficulty may be experienced in removing piston rings which have become badly gummed up with burnt oil, and if it is obvious that new rings will be needed (i.e. if they have become scorched or otherwise damaged) it is a waste of time endeavouring to remove them intact. Snap them off and prise off the broken pieces with a thin-edged tool such as that shown in Fig. 9. On rare occasions the top ring becomes so carbonized up that it has to be broken off, and occasionally piston rings on an aluminium alloy piston become stuck due to a partial or complete piston seizure, and to free them it is necessary to remove the smearing over the edges of the rings from the lands between. To do this, use a very fine file and remove only the barest amount of metal with the utmost care. If the smearing is extensive, there is no satisfactory remedy except to scrap the piston and fit a new one.

Most cases of stuck piston rings, however, are due to carbon

DECARBONIZING AND VALVE GRINDING

deposits in the grooves (caused generally by loose rings), and the piston should be immersed and allowed to soak in a paraffin bath until the carbon has become softened. It is probable that even after this treatment some trouble will be experienced in removing the rings, and the author strongly advocates the use of a tool such as that shown in Fig. 9 to ease them off. After slipping one end of the ring through the rectangular hole, the pointed end should be run around the groove under the stuck ring until it is completely freed. Do not use a screwdriver or chisel as the groove edges are very likely to be damaged.

Cleaning and Refitting Rings. The piston rings are the mainguard of engine compression and must be full of spring and free in their grooves. The rings on examination should be polished around

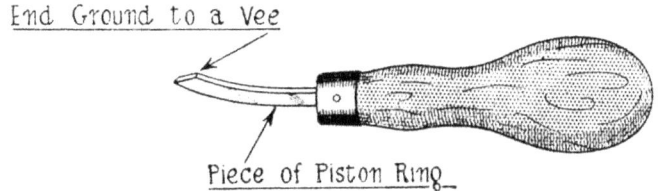

Fig. 10. A Home-made Tool for Cleaning Piston Ring Grooves

the whole of their surfaces, and if any ring has a brownish discoloration or a black patch on it, indicating gas leakage, it should be replaced by a new ring. Having removed the piston rings (it is considered good practice to leave them alone unless appreciable carbon deposits have formed in the grooves or the rings are gummed up), the piston should be washed in paraffin so that the extent of the carbon deposits can be readily seen. All carbon should be scraped from the backs of the rings, from the ends of the rings and from the ring grooves. Various proprietary scrapers are available for removing carbon deposits in the ring grooves and have the advantage that in one operation the carbon can be scraped from the three sides and corners of each groove.

Quite a good scraper can be made from a narrow wood chisel, but it must be of just the right size. It is also possible to make an excellent scraper by grinding the end of a small file or the end of a piece of broken piston ring which is, of course, of exactly the correct width. The piece of ring can then be mounted in a handle as shown in Fig. 10. Be exceedingly careful when scraping the carbon off not to injure the surfaces of the grooves or some loss of compression may follow and perhaps the piston may be irretrievably ruined. In addition to being free from carbon, the piston rings must be free to move in their grooves without much up and down play (0·002 in.–0·005 in. in the case of new rings) and their gaps should not exceed 0·020 in. A fair average gap for most engines is 0·003 in. per inch of bore diameter (see pages 63-4). With new rings the gap should be 0·008 in.–0·012 in. After the carbon has been removed from the piston rings, both the rings and piston should again be cleaned in paraffin and wiped dry with a non-fluffy rag. The piston rings should be refitted in exactly the same position as they were originally, and before replacing them with the aid of strips of tin (Fig. 8) or by replacing the top ring first followed by the others, place a few spots of oil in the grooves. See that the piston ring slots are opposite each other. On a three-ring piston space the ring slots at 120 degrees, and on a two-ring piston space them at 180 degrees.

Decarbonizing Piston and Cylinder. When decarbonizing, it pays to do the job as thoroughly as possible because carbon deposits form less quickly on smooth and polished surfaces. With a flat scraper, such as a blunt screwdriver, remove every trace of carbon from the top of the piston crown, taking great care in the case of an aluminium alloy piston not to exert excessive pressure, otherwise the comparatively soft metal may be scratched deeply. Removal of the piston from the connecting-rod unquestionably facilitates thorough cleaning and it also enables the underside of the crown to be scraped and the piston rings, if necessary, removed and the grooves cleaned, as previously described. The author, however, would emphasize that it is quite unnecessary to touch the rings more often than about every 5000 miles and even then it is not advisable to remove them unless substantial deposits in the grooves are preventing the rings from doing their duty properly. Do not attempt to remove any carbon from the lands between the grooves. After decarbonizing the piston clean it all over with paraffin and then polish the top of the crown with emery cloth or metal polish in the case of cast-iron and aluminium alloy pistons respectively. Finally remove every trace of abrasive by wiping with a rag damped in paraffin, and oil the piston after refitting it to the connecting-rod.

To decarbonize the combustion chamber, turn the cylinder or cylinder head upside down and then scrape off all carbon deposits with a blunt screwdriver or other scraper. The job is greatly facilitated if the head is held securely and a good method of doing this is to screw an old sparking plug into the head and grip this with a vice. An even better method is to obtain a piece of hexagon steel bar about 5 in. long and get one end turned and threaded to fit the sparking plug hole. The bar can then be placed upright between the vice jaws as shown in Fig. 11.

When chipping off the carbon deposits from the combustion chamber of a side-valve engine without a detachable head a long

DECARBONIZING AND VALVE GRINDING

scraper must be used, and great care should be taken not to let the shank touch the highly polished sides of the cylinder. Avoid deeply scratching the walls of the combustion chamber. On most engines some carbon forms on the slight ridge which is usually found inside the cylinder barrel at the top of the piston stroke, and such deposits should be cautiously removed. Next clean up the inlet and exhaust ports with a suitable scraper (special bent scrapers are sold for this purpose) and remove all carbon from the valve heads, valve caps (where fitted), and sparking plug (see page 47). If the silencer is choked and causing back-pressure,

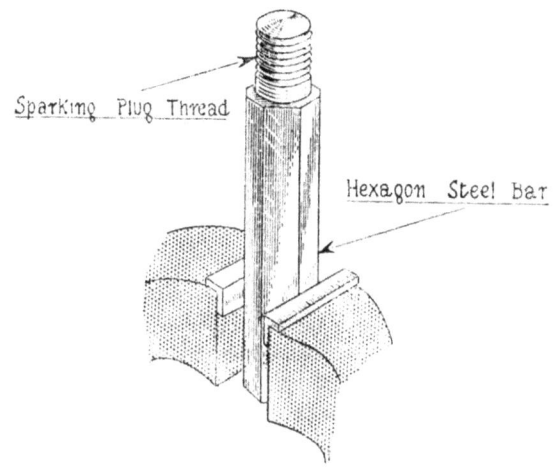

FIG. 11. A USEFUL GADGET FOR HOLDING THE CYLINDER HEAD WHILE DECARBONIZING

remove it and scour out all soot inside. After decarbonizing, wipe all the surfaces over with a rag damped in paraffin. If the engine has a detachable cylinder head, it is a good plan to polish the combustion chamber with emery cloth and engine oil, but, if this is done, the greatest care must be taken afterwards to remove all emery particles. Another method of polishing the combustion chamber and ports is to use riflers, but this type of polishing is rather in the nature of a refinement than a necessity, except perhaps when tuning a sports engine for maximum speed.

GRINDING-IN THE VALVES

It is inadvisable to grind-in the valves more frequently than every alternate decarbonizing unless some loss of compression occurs due to poor seating. It should be remembered, however, that, if the valves really do need attention and are neglected, both the valves and their seats may become damaged and refacing of the valves and recutting of the seats may be called for, an expensive operation.

If compression is good it should be possible to stand on the kick-starter of a motor-cycle for about twenty seconds without the engine commencing to turn over. Gas leakage past the valves is usually accompanied by slight hissing when turning the engine over against compression and it should be possible to detect the noise on listening close to the ports. Overheating and loss of power are present while running. Poor compression, on the other hand, may be due to one of a number of possible causes such as a sticking valve, a weak or broken valve spring, insufficient valve clearances, a defective cylinder-head joint, leaky valve caps, a damaged sparking plug washer, faulty piston rings, or a worn

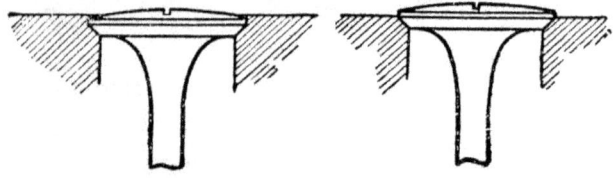

Fig. 12. Showing Why a Valve must not be Ground-in Excessively

The valve shown on the right is seating correctly, but that shown on the left has become "pocketed" due to too frequent or excessive grinding-in. "Pocketing" restricts the smooth and rapid entry and exit of gases past the valves and is detrimental to engine efficiency

piston and cylinder. Therefore, if loss of compression occurs, do not remove the valves immediately without taking other factors into consideration.

To Remove Side Valves. It is possible to remove the valves either with the cylinder in position or detached, but since removal of the cylinder enables the valves to be conveniently worked at on a bench or table, complete removal is advocated. First of all remove the valve caps (see page 14) or else take off the valve cover fitted to detachable head side-valve engines. To remove the valves it is necessary to compress the valve springs and withdraw the flat cotters (split collets on twin-cylinder V-type) from the slots in the ends of the valve stems. An excellent valve spring compressor for this purpose is the Terry illustrated in Fig. 13(A). To use this tool, place the hooked end over the top of the valve head and the forked end beneath the valve spring lower collar. Then lever each valve spring upwards by pressing down on the handle until the cotter can be pushed out. If stiff, gently tap it out, or pull it away with a pair of pliers. The valve spring, together with the two collars, can then be pulled off the valve stem and the valve drawn out from above. Be careful after removing the inlet and exhaust valves not to mix them up (see below).

To Remove Overhead Valves. With the detachable cylinder head removed and the rocker-box or rocker standard assembly taken off, it is a simple matter to remove the valves with a valve spring compressor such as the Terry shown in Fig. 13(B). On overhead-valve J.A.P. engines split collets are employed for anchoring the lower valve spring collars, and in order to remove the valves it

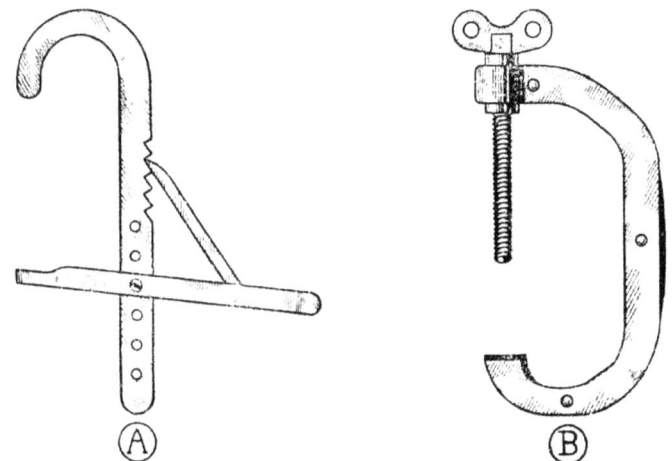

FIG. 13. SUITABLE VALVE SPRING COMPRESSORS FOR J.A.P. ENGINES

Both the tools illustrated are of Terry design. The lever type shown at *A* is suitable for side-valve engines and the screw type shown at *B* is for overhead-valve engines

is only necessary to place the forked end of the screw compressor under each lower valve spring collar and the pointed end of the screw in the centre of the valve head and screw up until the split collet can be removed and the collars and duplex springs taken off. Sometimes the collets are stiff and in this case tap them out. Before removing the valves take off the circlips (1932 on); be careful not to lose the hardened slip-on valve stem end caps.

Should no valve spring compressor be available, the following method can be employed for compressing the valve springs on side-valve or overhead-valve engines. Place some hard packing under the valve heads and place the cylinder or cylinder head so that the packing is flush with the bench. Then press down on the valve spring collars with a spanner or other suitable tool until the split collets are released. 1932 and later engines have a circlip in addition to split collets and this must first be removed from the valve stem. See also page 32.

Having removed the valves, care should be taken not to mix them because, although theoretically on some engines the inlet and exhaust valves are interchangeable, each valve is individually ground on to its seat and must be kept on this seat only to ensure a gastight seal. It is usually possible to identify the valves easily by reason of the fact that the exhaust valve becomes more highly discoloured than the inlet valve. Clean the valves with paraffin and wipe them dry. Then carefully inspect the valve heads and stems for carbon deposits and scale which should be removed without scratching the valves. Finally, polish the valve stems lengthwise with some worn emery cloth and polish the heads and necks with metal polish.

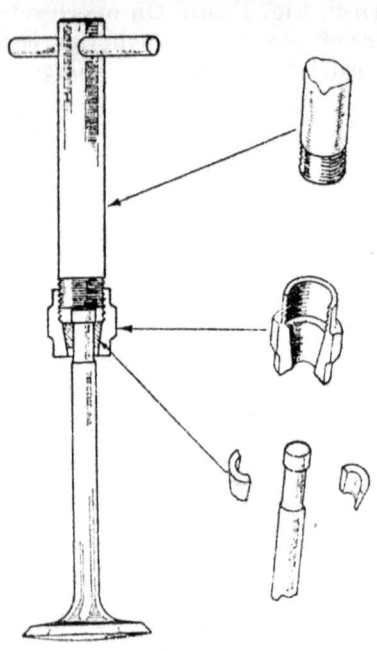

Fig. 14
J.A.P. Valve Grinding Tool for O.H.V. Engines

Test Valve Guides for Wear. It is not always realized that worn valve guides (especially a worn inlet guide) cause heavy petrol consumption, erratic slow running, and difficult starting. Before grinding-in the valves it is advisable to test the guides for wear by refitting the valves in the guides and trying to "rock" them sideways. If much wear is apparent, the guides should be renewed. (See page 140.)

Grinding-in the Valves. Examine the bevelled valve faces and their seats carefully for pitting which must be removed by grinding-in. The mushroom-headed valves on J.A.P. side-valve engines have slots in their heads to fit a screwdriver or bit held in a brace, but the valves on the Standard, Sports, and "high camshaft" O.H.V.s are not slotted and it is necessary to use a special valve-grinding tool. The tool shown in Fig. 14 is extremely handy and very simple to use. To grip the valve, place the split collet on the valve stem, slip the tool over it and tighten up the nut.

There are a number of good proprietary grinding pastes, such as Richford's, available, and these are often supplied in round tins

DECARBONIZING AND VALVE GRINDING

with two compartments, one having a fine grade paste, and the other a coarse paste which should be used only when the pitting is extensive or for making a preliminary rough cut. Fine carborundum or emery powder mixed with petroleum jelly or engine oil makes a useful grinding paste, but the ready-made compound is preferable.

To grind-in a valve hold the cylinder or cylinder head firmly on a bench or in a vice (see page 24), and after cleaning both the valve seat and valve, smear with a piece of rag or the finger tip a thin film of grinding paste (coarse first if dealing with an exhaust valve) on the valve face and replace the valve in its guide minus the valve spring. Before inserting it, however, it is a good plan on side-valve engines to insert a small spring between the valve head and valve guide to avoid the necessity of frequently lifting the valve off its seat by hand in order to turn it round, which is necessary to avoid the formation of grooves or rings on the valve face while grinding-in.

When grinding-in, a steady pressure on the grinding tool is required and care must be taken not to rock the valve, particularly if the valve guide is somewhat worn. Rotate the valve about *a third of a turn* in one direction and then an equal amount in the opposite direction, pausing about every half-dozen oscillations to raise the valve from its seat and turn it one-third to a quarter of a revolution. Cease grinding-in when no "cut" can be felt (and the valve begins to "sing") and put some more paste on the bevelled edge of the valve face if after cleaning the valve in paraffin some pitting is still visible. Continue grinding-in until both the valve face and seat have a matt ring over a considerable depth (line contact is not sufficient) and there are no pit marks left on wiping the paste off. Do not continue grinding-in after a good seating has been effected, because as has already been explained on page 26 excessive grinding-in eventually leads to the valves becoming "pocketed," which causes a considerable decline in power output. After grinding-in the inlet and exhaust valves wipe both the valves and their seats thoroughly clean with a paraffin- or petrol-soaked rag to ensure that there is absolutely no trace of any abrasive left.

Refitting Valves. After grinding-in the valves you should reassemble them in the cylinder head. Smear the valve stems with oil and replace them in their guides. Then refit the valve springs and collars, being careful not to mix up the upper and lower collars. Next compress each valve spring with the valve spring compressor and refit the split collet or cotter (first replace circlips on early O.H.V.s). The application of a little grease to the lower part of the valve stem facilitates reassembly on O.H.V. engines, as this enables the split collet to stick on the valve stem while compressing the springs. On O.H.V. engines do not forget to replace the hardened valve stem end caps, and if these are seriously worn, renew, otherwise side thrust will be imposed by the rockers on the valves and the guides will wear. On S.V. engines the valve caps (where fitted) may now be replaced.

After Reassembly. Where a detachable head is fitted, it is an excellent plan to test the seats by pouring some petrol into the ports and watching for leakage past the valves. Not the slightest sign of moisture should creep past the valves until after a considerable time has elapsed. If some petrol quickly gets past the valves it is sure proof that the valves have not been sufficiently ground-in and the remedy is (horrible thought!), remove and continue grinding-in. The ultimate test of good valve seating is engine compression.

Cleaning Cylinder Exterior. Rain and heat quickly cause the cylinder fins of an air-cooled engine to become rusty. This does not appreciably affect the running, but it becomes an eyesore, and to a small extent reduces heat radiation. To remedy this, clean the cylinder fins with a stiff brush soaked in paraffin, and afterwards paint the fins with cylinder black which can be obtained at most accessory dealers (see page 138).

Refitting Piston and Cylinder. This should be done in the reverse order of dismantling. Smear both the piston and inside of the cylinder with engine oil and refit the piston the correct way round (page 21) on the connecting-rod, pushing the gudgeon-pin, which should also be oiled, home from the side where the circlip has been removed. Fit a new circlip on this side (unless you are sure the old one is perfect) and see that it beds down properly in the piston boss groove and is fully expanded. Remember that if a circlip "goes west" with the engine running you may have to put your hand in your pocket for a new piston and cylinder. Also see that the cylinder barrel spigot and mouth of the crankcase are scrupulously clean, and smear a little gold size on the cylinder base or crankcase face.

To replace the cylinder put the piston well down, space the rings properly (see page 24), hold the cylinder over the piston with one hand and offer the piston up to it with the other, squeezing the rings (without upsetting the position of the gaps) together until the complete piston enters the cylinder. Avoid putting any side strain on either the piston or connecting-rod. After seeing that the spigot beds down on the crankcase squarely and closely, tighten up the cylinder nuts finger-tight first and then securely with a spanner in a diagonal order. Even tightening is important, otherwise there is some risk of distorting the cylinder flange and preventing its bedding down properly on the crankcase. Similar care must be exercised when tightening the cylinder-head bolts.

DECARBONIZING AND VALVE GRINDING

Replacing Cylinder Head. It is important before replacing the cylinder head on O.H.V. engines and side-valve engines with a detachable head to see that the cylinder and head faces are quite clean and that the copper gasket is perfect. Should the gasket show any indications of "blowing" having occurred, it should be replaced by a new one or else annealed by heating it to a dull red and immersing in cold water. No jointing compound is needed but it is essential to see that the head beds down squarely on the cylinder barrel spigot. Having carefully replaced the head, tighten down the fixing bolts diagonally with the special spanner.

Reassembling Overhead Valve Gear. This is quite straightforward and should present no difficulty. First turn the engine over until the piston is in a position such that both cams are in the "neutral" position and then proceed to replace the various parts in the reverse order of dismantling. On 1927-8 engines with open type rocker gear replace the rockers by screwing the spindles into the rocker standards and secure with the lock-nuts and split-pins. By levering the valves open, the push-rods can then be located between the ball ends of the rocker-arm adjusters and the cam levers.

In the case of 1929 and subsequent O.H.V. engines refit the complete rocker-box with the two securing bolts and replace the push-rods and covers, levering each valve open and pressing down on the push-rod cover against the lower spring until it fits into the rocker-box spigot. Make sure that both push-rods are snugly located in the cam lever recesses and that the loose balls in the upper push-rod ends engage the cupped rocker-arm adjusters. The oil pipes to the back of the rocker-box and the pipes to the valve guides (where fitted) may now be reconnected and the rocker-box end cover replaced. Before doing this, however, the valve clearances (see page 34) will require adjusting.

The rocker-box and cylinder head are integral on the "high camshaft" engines and so are replaced together, and the four bolts done up tightly. Flat-base tappets are provided on these engines and with the tappets slackened off it is a simple matter to refit the push-rods. See that the gland nut at the base of the telescopic push-rod cover tube is firmly retightened after final adjustment of the tappets (see page 34).

Completing Reassembly. Replace the sparking plug, carburettor petrol pipe, exhaust pipe(s), and also the petrol tank if this has been removed. Renew any washers whose condition is doubtful, and before refitting the plug see that it is clean and properly adjusted (page 47). On side-valve engines refit the valve covers and on overhead-valve engines the valve spring covers (where fitted). On "high camshaft" engines reconnect the exhaust valve lifter wire at the rocker-box and if necessary adjust the cable stop screw (page 38). The engine is now again ready for active service and it should prove very much more lively and flexible than it was prior to decarbonizing and grinding-in the valves. After a short mileage has been covered, go over the various engine nuts and bolts with a spanner and tighten any which can be turned the slightest fraction. Also recheck the valve clearances and adjust the tappets or rocker-arm adjusters if necessary.

Decarbonizing Hints (1939-52 500/600 c.c. O.H.V.). Most of the advice given in this chapter is applicable, but dismantling procedure is somewhat different. First remove the carburettor, sparking plug, exhaust pipe, etc. Then disconnect the rocker-box oil pipes and proceed to remove the rocker-box cover, being careful not to damage the washer. Now lever up the inner rocker-arms and pull the push-rods away from the rocker-box. When doing this, be careful not to lose the steel balls in the upper push-rod cups. Having removed the push-rods, undo the inverted cylinder-head nuts with a standard $\frac{3}{8}$ in. J.A.P. spanner, and remove the one-piece cylinder head and rocker-box. A gasket is provided and must be handled with care. In order to inspect the piston, remove the cylinder also as described on page 20, after undoing the base nuts. There is no base washer. The piston and rings may be dealt with as described on pages 20-4. Note that the piston requires heating to remove the gudgeon pin, and that the correct gap for the three rings is 0·010 in. Decarbonize thoroughly (see page 24).

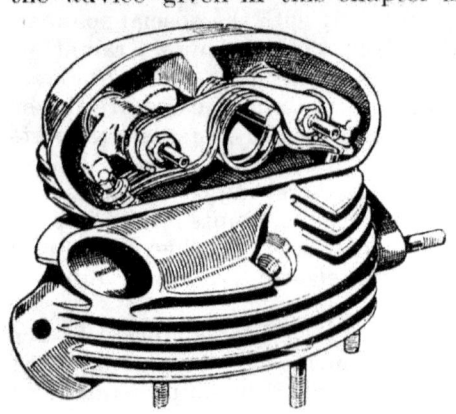

FIG. 15. CYLINDER HEAD AND O.H. VALVE GEAR ON 1939-52 500 C.C. AND 600 C.C. ENGINES
(*By courtesy of " Motor Cycling "*)

If it is desired to grind-in the valves, the valve springs must be compressed and the O.H. rockers dismantled, as described on page 33. When removing the valves, note that the exhaust valve has the larger head. Replace the push-rods with the cylinder.

Spares and Accessories. On page 139 are mentioned some firms who stock J.A.P. engine spares, tools, and miscellaneous accessories, including tools for decarbonizing, valve grinding, etc.

CHAPTER III

ADJUSTMENTS AND OVERHAUL

IN this chapter it is proposed to deal with various routine adjustments and overhauling (singles and Vee-twin engines), except lubrication, decarbonizing. For S.V. vertical twin, see page 67.

VALVE CLEARANCES

Adjustment is not often called for except in the case of a new engine where the valves tend to bed down for a time.

To Adjust Tappets (S.V. Engines). On all side-valve engines, including 1939-50 250 c.c. models, correct tappet clearances are 0·004 in. for the inlet valve and 0·006 in. for the exhaust valve. In every case the clearances should be checked and if necessary adjusted with the engine *cold*. To check the clearances, remove the valve cover (where fitted), turn the engine over until both valves are fully closed, and then insert a feeler gauge of the correct thickness between each tappet head and foot of the valve stem (Fig. 16). If the clearance is not as it should be, loosen the lock-nut *A* and then screw the tappet head *B* up or down with a spanner until the correct clearance is obtained. To prevent the tappet itself from rotating while making the adjustment, hold the hexagon *C* with another spanner. Then retighten the lock-nut securely and again check the tappet clearance. The clearances in the case of both inlet and exhaust tappets should be adjusted closely.

To Adjust O.H. Rockers (1939-52 500/600 c.c. O.H.V.). Valve clearance for both valves should be *nil with the engine cold*. To check the clearances, undo the hexagon nuts and remove the aluminium cover from the rocker-box (be careful with the paper washer), and "feel" the rockers after making sure that both valves are fully closed and the exhaust valve lifter adjustment is correct (see page 37). An eccentric sleeve is provided on each rocker spindle for adjustment (see Fig. 33); and to take up excessive valve clearance loosen the two lock-nuts which bear against the valve spring plate (Fig. 15), and then turn the knurled rim of the rocker sleeve (behind the plate) *anti-clockwise* for the inlet valve and *clockwise* for the exhaust valve. Afterwards retighten the lock-nuts and again "feel" the rockers.

To Remove O.H. Rockers. Remove the rocker-box cover and then take away the two outer cantilever valve springs by levering their ends until the split collets are freed from the valve stem collars. The springs may readily be slipped off the valve spring pin. Now remove the two nuts and take off the valve spring plate. Having done this, proceed to remove the inside valve springs similarly, and finally withdraw the rockers and sleeves.

To Adjust O.H. Rockers (1927-8 Engines). Tappets and ball-ended rocker screws have been employed on some 1927-8 J.A.P. Standard and Sports engines, but on the majority of O.H.V. engines direct acting push-rods with adjustable rocker screws are fitted. Where tappets are provided it is only necessary to loosen the lock-nuts and adjust the ball-ended rocker screws after first making sure that both valves are fully closed. The correct clearance for both the inlet and exhaust valves is 0·002 in. with the engine *cold* and this should be measured with a feeler gauge placed between the overhead rocker-arm pads and the valve stems or valve stem end caps (where fitted). The feeler should just "go" without binding.

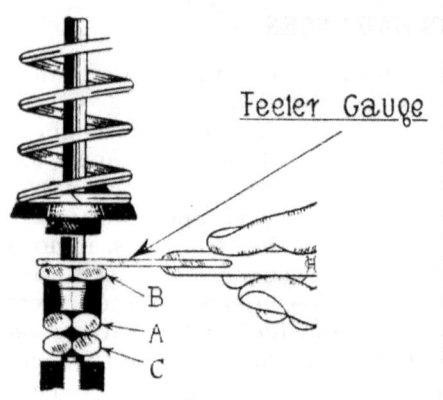

FIG. 16
CHECKING TAPPET CLEARANCE ON A S.V. ENGINE

Tappets are provided on the J.A.P. "high camshaft" engine, a part-sectioned drawing of which (with rocker-box cover removed) is shown in Fig. 17. As may be seen, rollers are fitted to the ends of the overhead rocker-arms and the valve clearances should be checked by slipping a suitable feeler gauge between the rollers and valve stem end caps after removing the rocker-box cover. With a *cold* engine the clearance for both valves should be 0·005 in. In order to gain access to the tappet heads and lock-nuts, unscrew the gland nut at the base of the large push-rod cover tube and press the telescopic portion upwards until the tappets are exposed. After making the necessary tappet adjustment see that the tappet lock-nuts and also the gland nut are firmly retightened. On "high camshaft" engines the tappets are prevented from turning while making the adjustment, by an internal plate.

To Adjust O.H. Rockers (1929 Onwards). On O.H.V. engines (except 1939-52 500/600 c.c.) with direct-acting type of push-rod the valve clearances should be checked with the engine *cold* by applying a 0·002 in. feeler gauge between the valve stem end caps and overhead rocker pads after removing the valve spring covers

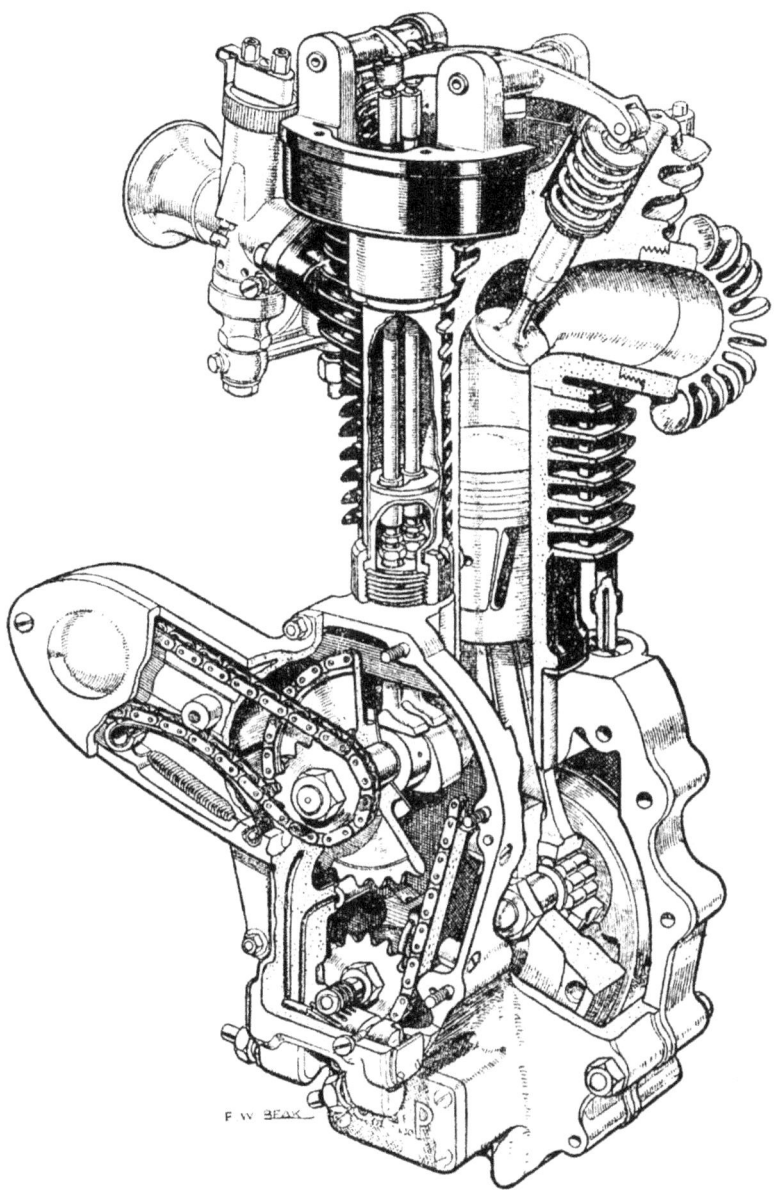

Fig. 17. "High Camshaft" Engine (1938 Onwards)
Showing tappet adjustment and other details. The rocker-box cover has been removed
(*By courtesy of "The Motor Cycle"*)

(where fitted). To adjust the clearances it is necessary to remove the rocker-box cover and then after loosening each lock-nut (Fig. 18) to screw in or out with a spanner applied to the flats above the rocker-arm the adjuster screw into whose cupped base the loose ball at the top of the push-rod fits. Afterwards retighten the lock-nuts, again check the clearances, and refit the rocker-box and valve spring covers.

How to Take Up End Play in Rocker-box. To ensure precise and therefore efficient action of the valve mechanism on overhead-valve engines it is important that there should be no appreciable end play of the rockers in the rocker-box. Should end play

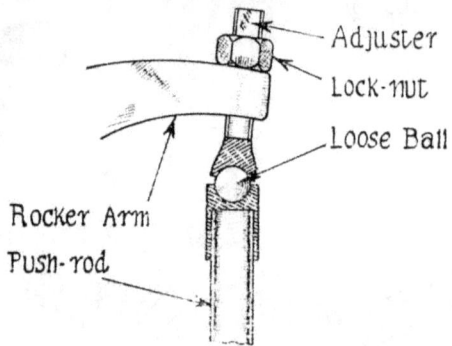

Fig. 18. Valve Clearance Adjustment Provided on Most O.H.V. Engines

exceeding $\frac{1}{64}$ in. develop after a considerable mileage has been covered, it may readily be taken up in the following manner. Remove the rocker-box from the cylinder head and take off the end cover. Then unscrew the four $\frac{1}{4}$ in. clamping nuts on the top of the rocker-box and, holding the rocker-box face downwards, deliver a sharp blow on the face at each end. This should cause the needle roller races (see Fig. 19) to move outwards slightly and stand proud of the face of the rocker-box. Now screw down the four $\frac{1}{4}$ in. clamping nuts finger-tight, carefully replace the end cover, and tighten down the lever nut on the outside of the cover. Two small pads on the inside of the rocker-box cover press against faces machined on the rocker-arm bosses and, therefore, should the bearing races have moved outwards too far when tapping the face of the rocker-box as previously described, the act of retightening the lever nut should locate them correctly, provided the four clamping nuts are done up only finger-tight. If necessary, tap the rocker-box cover gently. Finally retighten the clamping nuts very securely and see that the lever nut is locked home so that it is off vertical 30 degrees or more to the right. From previous

ADJUSTMENTS AND OVERHAUL

remarks it will be readily appreciated that when testing for end play of the overhead rockers the rocker-box cover must be kept tight against the face of the rocker-box.

Exhaust Valve Lifter Adjustment. On all except the "high camshaft" J.A.P. engines the exhaust valve lifter is screwed on to the left-hand side of the timing case and details of its design and method of working are clearly shown in Fig. 20. The return spring as may be seen is situated at the base around the rod to the arm on the cam spindle crank and as regards adjustment

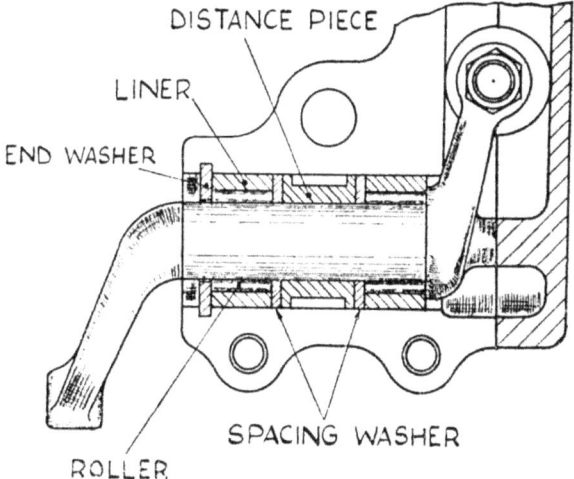

Fig. 19. Showing Method of Mounting Overhead Rockers in Rocker-box (most O.H.V. Engines)

The above arrangement has been used since 1929. One-piece rockers with needle roller bearings are fitted

it is necessary to keep the two nuts B adjusted so that the resistance of the spring is felt immediately the exhaust valve lifter lever (at the handlebars) is operated. No backlash other than that provided in the exhaust valve lifter mechanism itself is needed.

On early type J.A.P. engines it is necessary to raise the exhaust valve lifter from the timing case before removing the cover, but on later engines this is quite unnecessary. Should it be necessary to detach the Bowden cable from the valve lifter, this can be done very easily in the following manner. Pull up the Bowden adjusters B, together with the member C into which the upper adjuster screws, until the knurled collar F is released, and remove the collar. Then slide the outer spacing sleeve E upwards over the wire until the wire nipple A can be slipped out of the slot in the brass yoke piece, which frees the cable completely.

On the "high camshaft" engines an entirely different design of exhaust valve lifter is fitted on the rocker-box cover as may be seen in Fig. 21. An unusual feature is that the Bowden wire and not the casing is anchored to the cylinder head at *A*. The exhaust lifter return spring comprises a spring-loaded plunger situated below the lever arm attached to the rocker-box cover. It is undesirable to maintain any backlash at the operating lever (on the handlebars), and any adjustment required to take up slack can be effected by loosening the lock-nut *B* and turning the adjustable casing stop *C* the necessary amount.

CARBURETTOR TUNING AND MAINTENANCE

Mixture Too Rich. A correct mixture gives the best all-round results. If the open exhaust port of an engine running on a correct mixture is observed, it will be noticed that the flame is of a *whitish-blue* colour and small. If the mixture is slightly rich more power may be obtained than where the mixture is correct and combustion complete, but the slight increase in power output is accompanied by some wastage of fuel and the exhaust is apt to be dirty and contains a considerable proportion of poisonous carbon monoxide gas (invisible). The exhaust flame (at an open port) is usually of a characteristic *yellow* colour. In the event of the mixture being very rich, loss of power develops, carbon deposits form rapidly, fuel consumption becomes very excessive, and general sluggishness in running becomes manifest, accompanied by a tendency for black smoke to issue from the exhaust, especially when the throttle is quickly opened. This is due to fine carbon deposits forming and being blown out from the combustion chamber. Where the mixture is very rich a slight closing of the air lever is apt to choke the engine. An over-rich mixture sometimes causes a tendency for eight-stroking and if the mixture

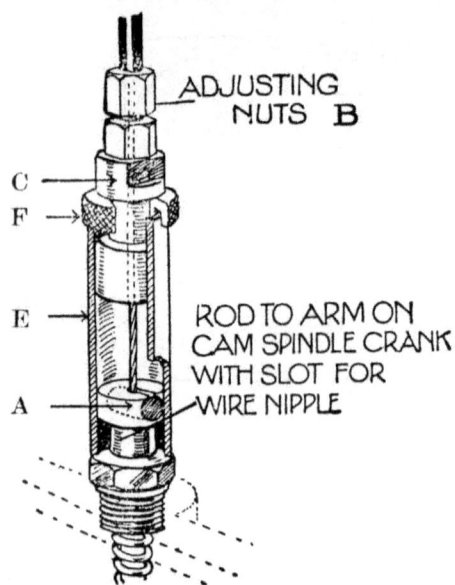

Fig. 20. Details of the Exhaust Valve Lifter Used on most Engines (not "High Camshaft")

ADJUSTMENTS AND OVERHAUL

is very rich the speed of the engine does not increase beyond a certain point in the throttle opening. Misfiring may occur. Possible causes of an excessively rich mixture are—
1. Incorrect carburettor adjustment (see pages 41-7).
2. Flooding of the carburettor (see Fig. 22).
3. Sticking of the air slide.
4. Faulty control adjustment.
5. A choked air intake gauze (when fitted).

A Weak Mixture. A rather weak mixture provides the most economical running and a clean exhaust, but the power output and maximum speed are not so good as where the mixture is correct or a little rich. The colour of the exhaust flame is *light blue*. Should the mixture be very weak, the power output is poor, overheating is apt to occur, slow-running is bad, misfiring may arise and the general performance of the engine is sluggish, accompanied usually by some popping back in the carburettor and hesitation in picking up which disappears as the air lever is closed slightly. Quite apart from the question of putting up with indifferent engine performance, it is most unwise to continue to run

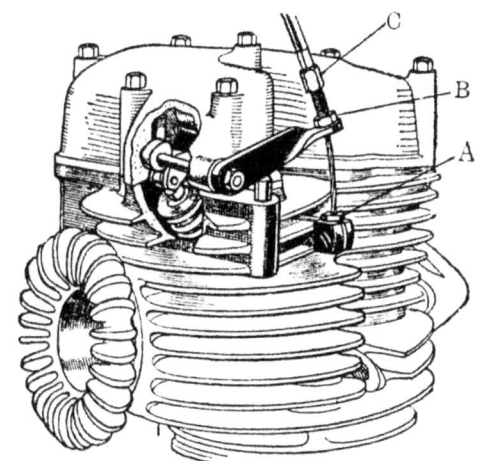

FIG. 21. EXHAUST VALVE LIFTER ON "HIGH CAMSHAFT" ENGINE
(*From "The Motor Cycle"*)

an engine on a weak mixture which has a slow rate of combustion and is still burning when ejected past the exhaust valve. Slow combustion which also occurs with an over-rich mixture is liable to cause overheating and damage the exhaust valve and its seat, and also to ignite the incoming mixture thereby causing popping back. Possible causes of a weak mixture are—
1. Incorrect carburettor adjustment (see pages 41-7).
2. Air leaks at inlet valve guide, carburettor slides, butterfly valve, or induction pipe.
3. Loss of compression (see page 26).
4. A choked jet, filter, or other stoppage in carburettor.
5. A stoppage in the petrol pipe.
6. Badly adjusted carburettor controls.

Difficult starting and poor slow-running are sometimes caused through badly seating valves or some defect in the ignition system such as a dirty or incorrectly adjusted plug (see page 47), a contact-breaker needing attention, or excessively advanced ignition timing; it is therefore wise to give the ignition system "the once-over" before suspecting faulty carburation.

Defective Float Chamber Needle. Dirt or grit may become lodged

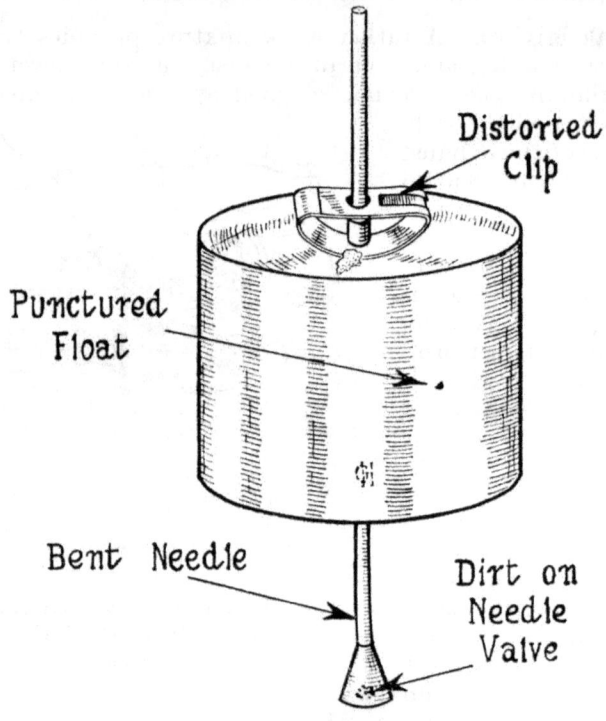

FIG. 22. SOME POSSIBLE CAUSES OF PERSISTENT CARBURETTOR FLOODING

between the float chamber and the needle valve, in which case the symptoms vary from mild flooding of the carburettor to profuse flooding. The remedy is to clean the needle seating and also thoroughly clean the inside of the float chamber. If the needle is bent, it should be replaced, but if it is seating badly the needle valve and seat should be polished by pulling the valve against its seat and rotating the needle with the fingers until a bright line contact is obtained, care being taken to keep the needle quite vertical.

ADJUSTMENTS AND OVERHAUL

Petrol Blown from Air Intake. This trouble, known as "popping back," is sometimes accompanied by a small blue flame, and loss of power, overheating, heavy fuel consumption and a characteristic noise are other objectionable symptoms. In the event of the carburettor catching on fire, instantly turn off the petrol and open the throttle wide so as to use up the petrol in the float chamber. Very slight "popping back" normally occurs on some high-efficiency engines and can be disregarded. The trouble may be due to a weak mixture which should be cured by strengthening the mixture by remedying air leaks (according to the cause), tuning the carburettor, or improving compression, according to what is at the root of the trouble.

If the inlet valve spring is weak, renew it, and if the ignition timing is excessively advanced, retard it slightly.

Tuning the Amal Carburettor. The standard setting is usually entirely satisfactory, but better results and more power may *sometimes* be obtained by the use of a slightly larger main jet or by making other adjustments. Various size jets are obtainable from Amal spare parts stockists, Messrs. Amal, Ltd., Writers, Ltd., or from the motor-cycle manufacturer (see also page 103).

Should the setting of this instrument not give entire satisfaction for particular requirements, there are four separate ways of rectifying matters as given herewith, and the adjustments should be made in this order: (*a*) Main jet ($\frac{3}{4}$ to full throttle); (*b*) pilot air adjustment (closed to $\frac{1}{8}$ throttle); (*c*) throttle valve cut-away on the air intake side ($\frac{1}{8}$ to $\frac{1}{4}$ throttle); and (*d*) needle position ($\frac{1}{4}$ to $\frac{3}{4}$ throttle). The diagram (Fig. 24) clearly indicates the part of the throttle range over which each adjustment is effective.

(*a*) To obtain the correct main jet size, several jets should be experimented with, and that selected should be the *one which gives maximum power and speed* on full throttle with the air lever three-quarters open. If maximum speed is the chief consideration, the jet size should be selected with the air lever fully open. For touring, to determine whether the jet is too large or too small, with throttle fully open, gradually close the air lever. If an increase in power is noticed, the jet is on the small size. If, however, when the air lever is opened fully an increase of power is obtained, the jet is too large.

(*b*) To weaken slow-running mixture, screw pilot air adjuster outwards, and to enrich, screw pilot air adjuster inwards.

Screw pilot air adjuster home in a clockwise direction. Place gear lever in "neutral." Slightly flood the float chamber by gently depressing the tickler. Then set ignition at half advance, throttle approximately one-eighth open, close the air lever, start the engine, and warm up. After warming up, reduce the engine revolutions by gently throttling down. The slow-running mixture will

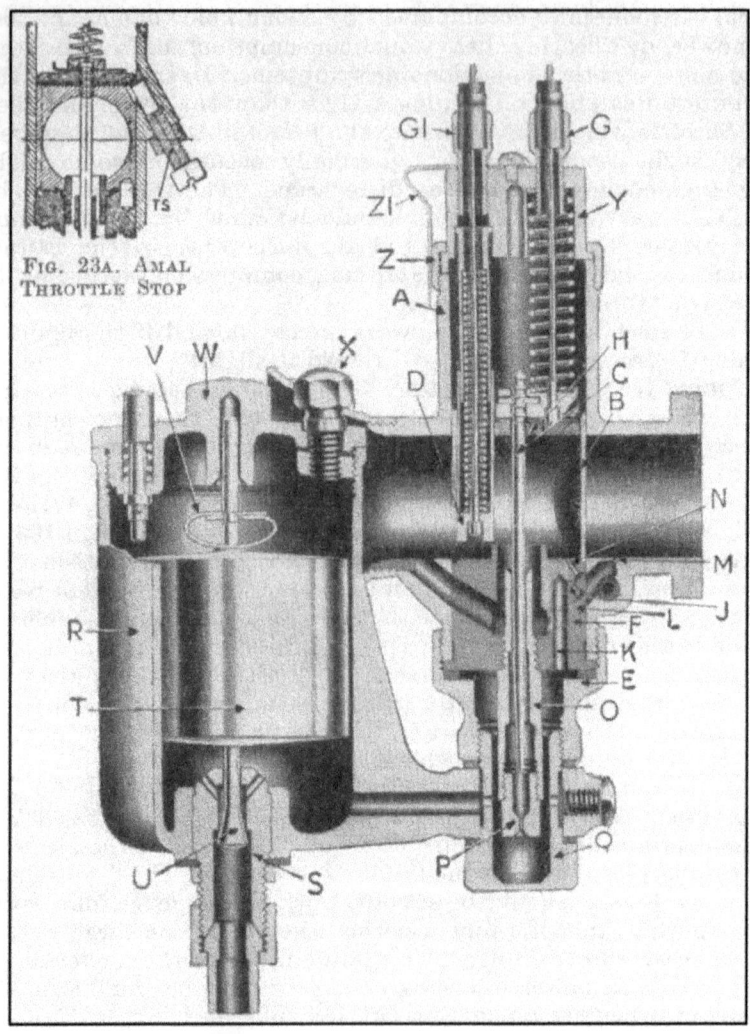

Fig. 23a. Amal Throttle Stop

Fig. 23. Sectional View of Amal Needle-jet Two-lever Carburettor Fitted on Many J.A.P. Engines

A flange fixing is generally used on O.H.V. engines and a clip fixing on certain S.V. engines. On some J.A.P. engines the Bowden carburettor (see Fig. 25) is fitted

ADJUSTMENTS AND OVERHAUL

prove over-rich unless air leaks exist. Very gradually unscrew the pilot jet adjuster. The engine speed will increase, and must again be reduced by gently closing the throttle until, by a combination of throttle positions and air adjustment, the desired "idling" is obtained. It is occasionally necessary to retard the ignition completely before getting a satisfactory tick-over, especially when early ignition timing is used. If it is desired to make the engine idle with the throttle quite closed, the position of the throttle valve must be set by means of the throttle stop screw, the throttle lever during this adjustment being pushed right home. Alternatively, if the screw is adjusted clear of the throttle valve,

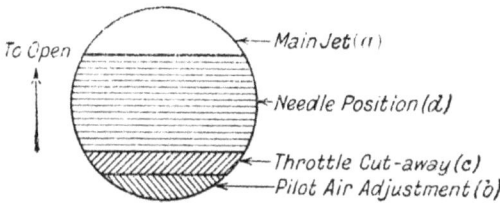

FIG. 24. RANGE AND SEQUENCE OF AMAL ADJUSTMENTS

the engine will be shut off in the normal way by the control lever.

(c) Given satisfactory "tick-over," set the ignition control at half-advance with the air lever fully open. Very slowly open the throttle valve, when, if the engine responds regularly up to one-quarter throttle, the valve cut-away is correct.

A weak mixture is indicated by spitting back through the air intake, with blue flames, and hesitation in picking up, which disappears when the air lever is closed down. This can be remedied by fitting a throttle valve with less cut-away. A rich mixture is shown by a black, sooty exhaust, and the engine falters when the air valve is closed. The remedy for this is a throttle valve with greater cut-away. Each Amal valve is stamped with two numbers, the first indicating the type number of the carburettor, and the second figure the amount of cut-away on the intake side of the valve in sixteenths of an inch, e.g. 6/4 is a type 6V. with a $\frac{4}{16}$ in. —i.e. a $\frac{1}{4}$ in—cut-away.

(d) Open air lever fully and the throttle half-way. Note if the exhaust is crisp and the engine flexible. Close the air valve slightly below the throttle, when the exhaust note and engine revolutions should remain constant. Should popping back and spitting occur with blue flames from the intake, the mixture is weak, and the needle should be slightly raised. Test by lowering the air valve gently. The engine revolutions will rise when the air valve is lowered slightly below the throttle valve. A 0·1065 is a standard needle-jet.

If the engine speed does not increase progressively with raising of the throttle, and a smoky exhaust is apparent with heavy laboured running, and tendency to eight-stroke, the mixture is too rich and the needle should be lowered in the throttle valve. After the correct needle position has been found, the carburettor setting is now complete, and it will be found that the driving is practically automatic once the engine is warmed up. For speed the main jet size may be increased by 10 per cent, when the air lever should be fully open on full throttle. If extreme economy is desired, lower the needle one groove farther after carrying out the above-mentioned four tests.

Maintenance of the Amal Carburettor. Periodical cleaning is necessary to maintain efficient functioning of the carburettor, and should be carried out in the following sequence.

Disconnect petrol pipe. Unscrew the jet plug Q (Fig. 23) and remove float chamber complete. With box or set spanner, slacken the mixing chamber union nut E. Mixing chamber complete may now be removed from engine, either by unscrewing the clip pin or flange screws holding the carburettor. Unscrew mixing chamber lock ring Z (held by clip $Z1$), and pull out throttle valve, needle and air valve. Remove main jet P and needle jet O. Mixing chamber union nut E may then be removed and jet block complete pushed out. If this is obstinate, tap gently, using a wooden stump inside the mixing chamber. Unscrew float chamber cover W after slackening lock screw X. Withdraw the float by pinching the clip V inwards, and pull gently upwards.

Generally it is sufficient to wash all parts in clean petrol, but if the carburettor has had extended service, check the following—

(a) FLOAT CHAMBER NEEDLE U. If a distinct shoulder is visible on the point of seating, renew this as soon as convenient.

(b) THROTTLE VALVE. Test in mixing chamber, and if excessive play is present it is advisable to renew this without delay.

(c) THROTTLE NEEDLE CLIP. This part must securely grip needle. *Free rotation must not take place*, otherwise the needle groove will become worn and necessitate a new part being fitted. *Be sure to refit the clip in the same groove.*

(d) JET BLOCK. If trouble has been experienced with erratic "idling," ascertain by means of a fine *bristle* that the pilot jet J is clear, and that the pilot outlet M in the mixing chamber is unobstructed.

The Bowden Carburettor. This instrument which has a butterfly throttle is made in two types. On type A the starting device is controlled from the handlebars by Bowden cable and on type B

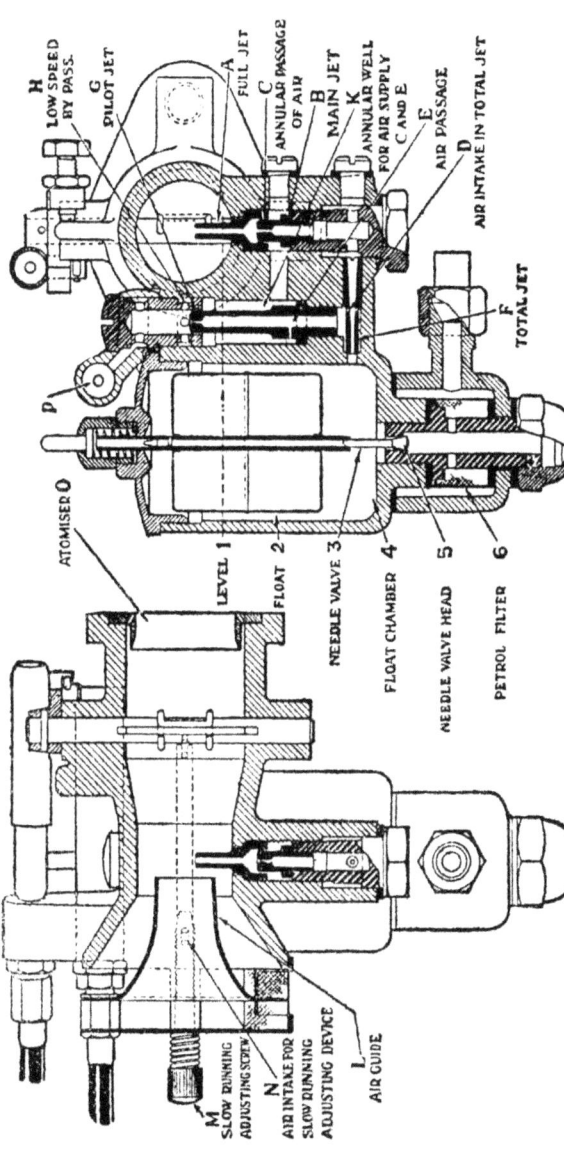

Fig. 25. Sectional Views of Bowden Carburettor
Every Bowden carburettor is supplied with two spare main jets

there is a knob control on the carburettor itself. The action of the carburettor is entirely automatic, the handlebar mixture control being brought into use for starting purposes only. Four jets are provided, namely (*a*) the pilot jet, (*b*) the main jet, (*c*) the total jet, (*d*) the full jet. It should be particularly noted that jets (*c*) and (*d*) are definitely fixed to suit the engine and must not be altered.

Tuning for Slow Running (Type A). To tune for easy starting from cold, first of all screw the adjusting screw M (Fig. 25) right in. Next, turn the twist-grip very slightly (about $\frac{1}{16}$ in.) so as to cause a big suction over the pilot jet G when the engine is started. Move the mixture control lever to the closed or starting position (unless the engine is warm), thereby closing the air intake situated at P. The effect of closing this air passage is to enrich the mixture delivered by the pilot jet G considerably, and a rich mixture is needed for starting from cold. Now retard the ignition lever and if the air temperature is very low, flood the carburettor (do not do so otherwise). The engine should then be kicked over.

After the engine has sprung into life, warm it up at a moderately fast pace and then move the mixture control lever to the normal position (which is open) and close the throttle right down by means of the twist-grip. Having done this the engine revolutions should be slowly reduced by unscrewing the throttle stop screw until a fair tick-over is obtained. The mixture will be found in most cases to be on the rich side, and eight-stroking and/or "hunting" may occur.

To Weaken the Mixture. In the event of the mixture being too rich and good slow-running unobtainable, unscrew the adjusting screw M so as to cause an air intake at N, the effect of which is to weaken the mixture and cause more even running and absence of "hunting." The engine revolutions will also increase slightly. It should be borne in mind, however, that it is futile to unscrew the screw M more than is necessary to uncover fully the air intake N.

Pilot Jet Size. Should a good tick-over not be obtained when the air intake N is fully opened, fit a slightly *smaller* pilot jet and screw in the adjusting screw M until perfectly even running results. Let us suppose that the engine stalls when the adjusting screw M is screwed fully home with the mixture control lever moved to the normal position. This indicates that the mixture is excessively weak and a *larger* pilot jet should be inserted.

It should be noted that on some models the location of the screw M is different from that shown in the sectional view of the type A carburettor, the screw being situated on the side of the carburettor opposite the throttle, and working in exactly the same way. This arrangement, however, causes the air intake N to

ADJUSTMENTS AND OVERHAUL

become superfluous and it is replaced by a similar air intake on the body of the air adjusting screw device. To obtain good tick-over, adjust the throttle stop screw carefully.

To Tune for Power (Types A and B). Most motor-cyclists are not so rich in these days that they can afford to get "power at any price," and therefore the smallest main jet should be fitted which gives plenty of power. If a road test reveals power in abundance, try the effect of fitting a main jet one size smaller. No loss of power may result and a considerable gain in miles per gallon may be obtained.

If the power output is none too good, try the effect of replacing the existing jet by one a size larger; it is highly probable that this will give maximum power combined with a low fuel consumption. When reducing the main jet size in order to obtain more economical running, bear in mind the possibility of too weak a mixture causing overheating and thereby upsetting the carburation. See also notes on page 107.

CARE OF IGNITION COMPONENTS

Suitable Lodge Plugs. Always run on the correct type of plug. Some J.A.P. engines take an 18 mm. size but most engines made since 1934 take a 14 mm. plug. Where the plug size is 18 mm., on all O.H.V. engines fit a Lodge H1, on S.V. engines a C3 is suitable. Where the plug size is 14 mm., a Lodge H14 should be used except in the 125 c.c. two-stroke where a C14 is recommended. For racing engines a special high heat-resisting plug such as a Lodge R49 is needed. For super-sports engines used for fast road work, fit a Lodge HHN or HNP plug (see also page 68).

Keep the Plug Gap Correct. Even on the most expensive plug the electrode points gradually burn away with the result that the gap between them becomes gradually enlarged. It is therefore advisable every few thousand miles, or whenever engine trouble develops, to remove the plug and check the gap at the electrodes with a feeler gauge, and if necessary bring the points closer together by pressing on the *side* earth electrode. With magneto ignition models, where the voltage depends to some extent on engine speed, if an excessive gap exists, difficult starting is likely to arise. With coil ignition models it is not so likely as the h.t. current is of practically constant voltage. For magneto and coil models the correct gap is about 0·018-0·020 in. and 0·020-0·022 in., respectively, except for racing plugs.

Clean It Frequently. The plug is liable to become oiled up (particularly during the running-in period), sooty or carbonized. Fortunately it is easy to clean, and as a dirty plug affects engine performance you should make a habit of removing the plug fairly frequently and cleaning it. If the plug is not very dirty it is usually sufficient merely to brighten up the electrodes where the spark occurs with the aid of a penknife. If the plug is very dirty it should be cleaned with petrol and a wire brush, both inside and outside. Special plug cleaners are available. To remove really thick deposits the plug should be dismantled, but if this is done see that the gland nut is firmly retightened. All deposits of carbon and soot must be completely removed. Examine the insulation for cracks or flaws. See also page 52.

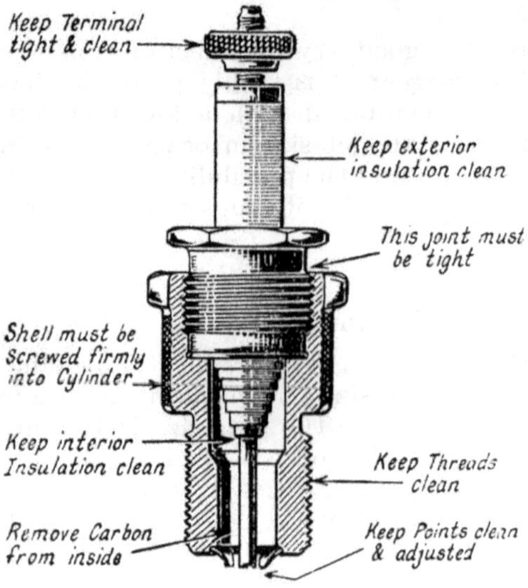

How to Test a Plug. If you have a neon tube plug tester it is only necessary to watch the flash in the little window of the tester. But if you have not got such a gadget, remove the plug with the h.t. lead attached, clean and adjust it as described above if necessary, and lay it on the cylinder head with the terminal clear and note whether it sparks correctly when the engine is rotated with the kick-starter. The spark though barely visible in broad daylight should be distinctly audible. On a twin-cylinder J.A.P. engine to determine which plug is faulty, short each in turn with a wooden-handled screwdriver with the engine running. As soon as the good plug is shorted the engine will stop or run extremely badly.

FIG. 26
PLUG MAINTENANCE AT A GLANCE

Keep Terminal tight & clean
Keep exterior insulation clean
This joint must be tight
Shell must be screwed firmly into Cylinder
Keep interior Insulation clean
Keep Threads clean
Remove Carbon from inside
Keep Points clean & adjusted

Contact-breaker Maintenance. A magneto, "Magdyno," "Maglita," or dynamo is best left well alone if it continues to function satisfactorily, but about every 1000-1500 miles the contact-breaker cover should be removed and the contact-breaker carefully inspected and, if necessary, adjusted. Contact-breakers (see Figs. 27 and 28) are broadly speaking of two types: (*a*) the stationary type in which the contacts and rocker-arm do not rotate, and (*b*) the rotating type in which the whole contact-breaker revolves. Possible sources of contact-breaker trouble are—

1. Sluggish action of the rocker-arm.

ADJUSTMENTS AND OVERHAUL

2. Incorrect adjustment of the contacts.
3. Pitted contacts.
4. Dirty or loose contacts.
5. Incorrect timing of the "break."

Sluggish Action. Correct adjustment and maintenance of the contact-breaker is most important. When the contacts are fully closed (i.e. when the rocker-arm heel or pad leaves the cam ring or cam) the fixed and adjustable contacts should be pressed firmly together by means of the spring. Sticking of the rocker-arm

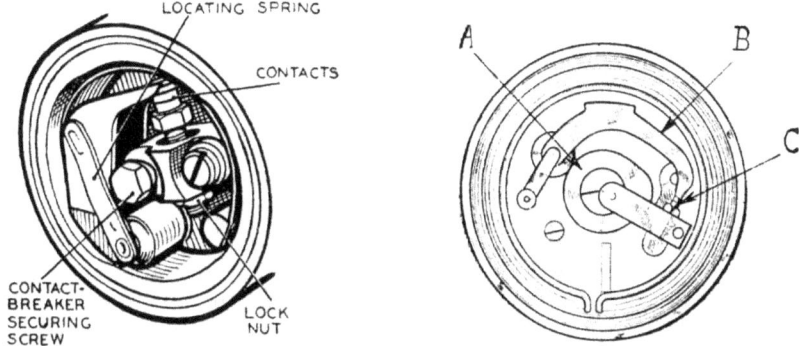

FIG. 27. ROTATING TYPE (LUCAS) AND STATIONARY TYPE (MILLER) CONTACT-BREAKERS

On the rotating type contact-breaker (left) the complete contact-breaker revolves, the rocker-arm being actuated by the stationary cam ring. On the stationary type only the cam revolves. At A, B, C are shown the cam, rocker-arm, and contacts respectively

on its pivot prevents a smart make-and-break and may give rise to erratic running of the engine. If the rocker-arm bush is of metal, polish and slightly oil both the rocker-arm bearing and the pivot pin, but if the bush is of fibre it should not be oiled; carefully ease it with emery cloth or a very fine round file. In damp weather fibre bushes sometimes swell slightly and oiling only makes matters worse. A dodge which often works is to rub the inside of the rocker-arm bush with the head of a live safety match. Should the contact spring break, a sudden and complete engine stoppage occurs and the remedy is to replace the spring or make a temporary repair with a small rubber band. Any sign of rusting on the contact-breaker spring should be seen to as breakage is sometimes due to gradual rusting.

In the case of the contact-breaker on a Lucas "Maglita," examine the plunger spring and control occasionally as rusting here may cause binding of the control and sticking of the tappet in its guide. On the stationary type of contact-breaker (e.g. Miller) petroleum jelly smeared on the cam is helpful and reduces wear on the rocker heel. For notes on lubrication see page 13.

The Correct Gap at the Contacts. It is advisable about every 1000 miles to remove the contact-breaker cover and check the gap between the fixed and adjustable contacts (with the contacts wide open) and make an adjustment if the gap varies *considerably* from the thickness of the feeler gauge provided on the contact-breaker spanner. For the Lucas "Magdyno" fitted to some machines the correct gap is about 0·012 in. On the Lucas "Maglita" the correct gap is 0·010 in., and this applies also to the contact-breaker fitted on the Lucas E3E dynamo. With Miller "Dyno-mags" gap is 0·016 in.–0·018 in. Where a Miller dynamo is concerned (coil ignition) the correct gap is 0·018 in.–0·020 in. (DHI: 0·022 in.). The correct gap for the Lucas and modern M-L magnetos is the same as for the magneto portion of the "Magdyno."

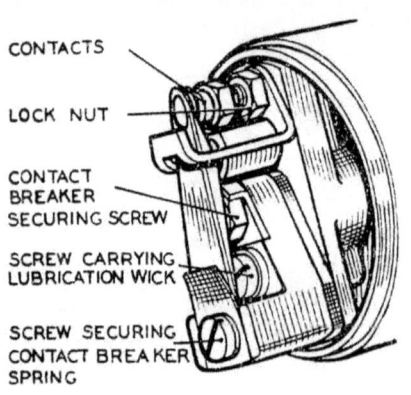

Fig. 28. Face Cam Type Contact-breaker Used on all Later Lucas "Magdynos" and Magnetos

The curved contact-breaker spring must always be fitted as shown

(*By courtesy of Joseph Lucas, Ltd.*)

It should be borne in mind that an excessive gap between the contacts does two things: (*a*) it reduces the period during which the primary circuit is closed; (*b*) it advances the ignition timing. Insufficient clearance may not only cause misfiring but is apt to cause pitting of the contacts due to sparking across them. Adjustment, however, is seldom called for provided the contacts are kept clean and free from oil (most important).

To Adjust the Gap. Turn the engine round slowly by hand until the contacts are wide open, and then with the small contact-breaker spanner loosen the lock-nut securing the adjustable contact and turn the contact screw until the feeler gauge on the spanner just enters without friction. Afterwards see that the lock-nut is securely retightened. This method of adjustment is applicable to most contact-breakers, but in the case of the Lucas E3E contact-breaker (a stationary type) the adjustment is made by loosening the screws holding the plate on which the stationary

ADJUSTMENTS AND OVERHAUL

contact is mounted and moving the plate until the correct gap between the contacts is obtained. Retighten the screws firmly.

Cleaning the Contacts. It is of vital importance *always* to keep the contact-breaker scrupulously clean and not to allow the slightest trace of oil to get on the contacts, otherwise they are very likely to become burnt and pitted. Bad pitting may also arise through a faulty condenser or, in the case of coil ignition models, loose battery connexions. Healthy contacts present a grey frosted appearance and their condition should be carefully noted from time to time. If the contacts are only slightly discoloured, it is generally sufficient to clean them with a rag or cloth moistened with petrol, but if they are found to be blackened

FIG. 29. WHAT TO AVOID WHEN TRUING UP CONTACTS
In the centre the contacts are shown correctly trued up. On the left and right are shown the results of carelessly using a file, the contact surfaces having become convex and out of parallel respectively
(*By courtesy of "The Motor Cycle"*)

or burned (probably due to oil or dirt), clean and polish the contacts first with *very fine* emery cloth and afterwards with a petrol-moistened cloth, being very careful to remove completely all traces of metallic dust and dirt. Clean any rust on spring.

Badly pitted or uneven contacts require to be very cautiously trued up and polished. The best method of cleaning up the contacts is to use a *very fine* carborundum slip. If this is not available, use *very fine* emery cloth. It is not advisable to use any kind of file.

Remove the slightest amount of metal, for remember the contacts are not made of cheap material and there is only a small thickness of it. Accurate truing up of the contacts is most important, and great care must be taken to see that the surfaces are not only smooth and bright but meet squarely (see Fig. 29). They must not be carelessly made non-parallel or convex. Unquestionably the contacts are most easily and accurately trued up by removing the rocker-arm from the contact-breaker. With the rotating contact-breaker (Fig. 27, left) the complete contact-breaker mechanism can be removed from its spindle after withdrawing the fixing screw, and the rocker-arm can then be readily prised off after pushing aside the locating spring. With the stationary contact-breaker (Fig. 27, right) it is quite easy to remove the rocker-arm and also the insulated contact mounting if necessary.

In the case of the M.L. magneto the spring blade carrying the moving contact should be detached as this makes both contacts very accessible. When reassembling, see that the small backing spring is replaced with its convex side next to the spring blade, otherwise a fracture may occur.

Where a Lucas face cam type contact-breaker (see Fig. 28) is concerned, to render the contacts accessible for cleaning, remove the spring arm carrying the moving contact by detaching the fixing screw. Finally check, adjust contact-breaker gap.

Loose Contacts and What to Do. The symptom is intermittent misfiring and the looseness is usually discernible to the eye. If the electrical contact is loose in the screw, the remedy is to get the contact soldered firmly in place by a jeweller (it is a delicate job). If the screw itself is loose, tighten the lock-nut.

Remove Pick-up Occasionally. About every 2000-3000 miles on magneto ignition models the H.T. pick-up (on twin-cylinder magnetos and "Magdynos" there are two) should be removed by releasing the securing clip or undoing the screws and the pick-up brush(es) and the slip-ring thoroughly cleaned. A pick-up brush may be cleaned by wiping with a cloth moistened in petrol, but if it is badly worn it should be renewed. See that the brush works freely in its holder and that the spring is not weak. Before replacing the pick-up wipe the moulding clean with a dry cloth and clean the slip-ring track and flanges of all carbon dust and oil by inserting a soft cloth through the pick-up hole and rotating the engine with the cloth pressed against the slip-ring with a suitable piece of wood.

Suitable K.L.G. and Champion Plugs. Recommendations for Lodge sparking plugs are given on page 47. Where K.L.G. plugs are used on J.A.P. engines, the following types are suitable. On S.V. engines requiring 18 mm. plugs, fit a K.L.G. M50 or a Champion 7. On S.V. engines designed to take 14 mm. plugs, fit a K.L.G. F50 or Champion L-10. On O.H.V. engines requiring 18 mm. plugs, use a K.L.G. M60 or a Champion 16 or 17. In the case of O.H.V. engines designed to take 14 mm. plugs, fit a K.L.G. F70 or a Champion L-10S. It should be noted that all sparking plug recommendations given on this and earlier pages apply to J.A.P. singles and Vee Twins, but *not* to the 494 c.c. S.V. vertical twin engine.

Cleaning Sparking Plugs. The importance of keeping the sparking plug clean inside and outside has already been mentioned on page 47. A useful gadget, obtainable from some accessory firms, comprises a metal reservoir containing petrol and steel

ADJUSTMENTS AND OVERHAUL

wires. The plug is screwed into the reservoir and then shaken. This provides a quick method of cleaning.

Lodge and K.L.G. sparking plugs are of the three-piece type and can readily be dismantled for thorough cleaning as shown in Fig. 30. Whenever a plug is very dirty, dismantle it by holding the hexagon of its body in a vice or suitable spanner and then unscrewing the gland nut with a box spanner. The insulated centre portion can now be detached. Lodge Plugs, Ltd., of Rugby, or K.L.G. Sparking Plugs, Ltd., of Cricklewood Works, London, N.W.2, or most good garages, can supply a suitable tool for dismantling plugs.

After dismantling a Lodge or K.L.G. sparking plug, clean the plug insulation (Sintox or Corundite respectively) by washing with petrol or with paraffin. Afterwards eradicate all soot and carbon deposits by using fairly coarse emery cloth or glass-paper. Then wash again the insulation with petrol or paraffin. Having

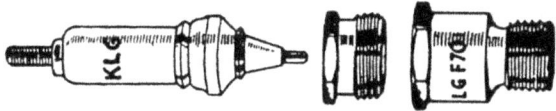

FIG. 30. K.L.G. SPARKING PLUG DISMANTLED FOR CLEANING

thoroughly cleaned the insulation, polish it with a soft, dry rag. Clean the centre electrode (except on a Lodge HNP plug) by polishing it with *fine* emery cloth. Next scrape all carbon deposits from the outer (earth) electrode and from the inside of the plug body, using a pocket-knife or wire brush. Finally rinse the plug body in petrol and allow it to dry. Before assembling the plug, verify that the internal washer in the plug body is seating properly, and see that there is no grit between the metal body and the centre insulator. The Champion Sparking Plug, Co., Ltd., of Feltham, Middlesex, advocate cleaning their non-detachable type plugs on a Champion Service Unit or by pouring some petrol into the space between the "Ceramic" insulator and the plug body and then setting the plug on fire to burn off deposits. With the larger plugs it is possible to clean the plug by inserting a piece of cloth between the insulator and body.

IGNITION AND VALVE TIMING

It is desirable to run with the ignition timed as closely as possible to the maker's setting and, of course, the valve timing must be absolutely accurate. However, it is seldom that the valve timing has to be disturbed, and to prevent any error in retiming a system of marking the timing wheels is employed.

Effect of Wrong Ignition Timing. Excessive spark advance is very bad for the engine and, besides causing difficult starting and poor slow-running, produces knocking under the slightest provocation. The big-end bearing is subjected to very unfair stresses and its life is shortened accordingly. On the other hand, if the spark is excessively retarded, loss of power will occur and also overheating and probably banging in the exhaust system. The exhaust port may get extremely hot and the valve become burnt.

Retiming the Ignition. There are two methods of doing this. One can use the piston stroke method or the degree system. The ignition advance for any particular engine is given in millimetres

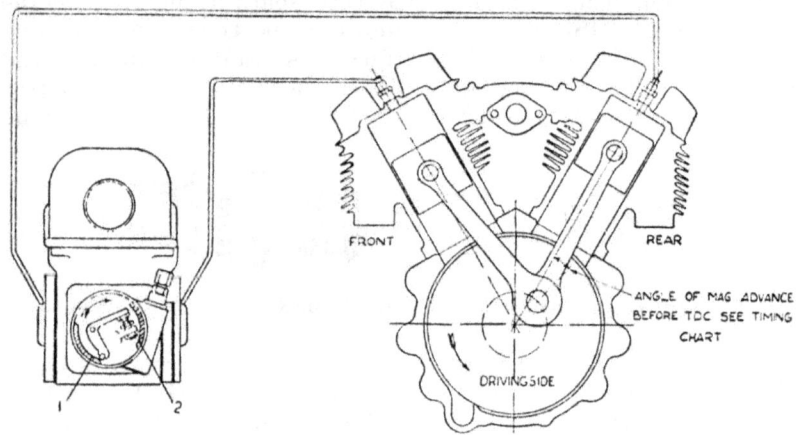

FIG. 31. IGNITION SETTING FOR VEE TWIN ENGINE
On twin-cylinder engines the ignition must be timed for the rear cylinder and the cam for this cylinder is No. 1

or degrees of crankshaft rotation before top dead centre (T.D.C.) on the compression stroke. For instance, on the Standard O.H.V. "500" the correct ignition advance is 17 mm. or 40 degrees before T.D.C. with the ignition lever fully *advanced*. For ordinary purposes a sufficiently accurate ignition timing can be obtained by using the piston stroke method which is more simple than the degree method where one has to attach a degree disk to the crankshaft as explained in a later paragraph dealing with valve timing. Using the piston stroke method, one needs a piece of stiff wire or a T.D.C. indicator (obtainable from most accessory dealers).

Timing on the Piston Stroke. To retime by the piston stroke method, first turn the engine over slowly by hand until the piston is at the top of the compression stroke (i.e. the upward stroke after the inlet valve has just closed) with both valves fully closed and the piston as near T.D.C. as possible. On side-valve engines

ADJUSTMENTS AND OVERHAUL

VALVE AND IGNITION TIMINGS FOR 1932-48 J.A.P. ENGINES

Pre-war engines continued for 1947-8 indicated thus: (1947-8)

TYPE OF ENGINE (See also pp. 59, 74-5, 142-3)	Inlet		Exhaust		Ignition
	Opens Before T.D.C.	Closes After B.D.C.	Opens Before B.D.C.	Closes After T.D.C.	Advance Before T.D.C.
150 c.c. S.V. Standard	15°	50°	50°	20°	35°
175 c.c. S.V. Standard (1947)					
200 c.c. ,, ,,					
250 c.c. ,, ,, (1947-8)					
300 c.c. ,, ,,	15°	50°	50°	20°	40°
350 c.c. ,, ,,					
350 c.c. S.V. Special					
350 c.c. ,, ,, Sports (1947)					
*350 c.c. ,, ,, ,, D.S.	23°	63°	65°	25°	40°
†350 c.c. ,, ,, ,, D.S.	25°	60°	65°	20°	40°
500 c.c. S.V. Standard (1947)					
550 c.c. ,, ,,					
600 c.c. ,, ,,					
600 c.c. S.V. (1947-8)	16°	65°	65°	25°	40°
600 c.c. ,, Sports					
500 c.c. ,, ,,					
500 c.c. ,, W/C					
600 c.c. ,, ,,					
680 c.c. S.V. Standard Twin					
750 c.c. ,, ,, ,, (1947)	18°	45°	60°	25°	40°
1100 c.c. S.V. W/C 60° Twin					
1100 c.c. ,, A/C ,, ,, (1947-8)					
1323 c.c. ,, ,, ,, ,, (1947-8)	16°	65°	65°	25°	38°
1100 c.c. O.H.V. W/C ,, ,,					
980 c.c. S.V. Twin	17°	65°	65°	25°	45°
175 c.c. O.H.V. Standard					
200 c.c. ,, ,,	27°	67°	67°	27°	45°
250 c.c. ,, ,, (1947)					
*350 c.c. O.H.V. Standard (1947)	23°	63°	65°	25°	45°
*350 c.c. ,, Special					
*500 c.c. O.H.V. Standard (1947)	22°	62°	65°	25°	40°
*500 c.c. ,, Sports					
*600 c.c. ,, Standard	22°	62°	65°	25°	45°
†350 c.c. ,, Standard	28°	55°	60°	20°	45°
†350 c.c. ,, Special					
†500 c.c ,, Standard	16°	65°	65°	25°	40°
†600 c.c. ,, ,,	16°	65°	65°	25°	45°
680 c.c. O.H.V. Std. Twin	23°	63°	65°	25°	45°
*1000 c.c. O.H.V. Std. Twin	25°	66°	65°	23°	45°
*175 c.c. O.H.V. Racing	27°	67°	67°	27°	45°
*250 c.c. O.H.V. Racing	27°	67°	67°	27°	45°
†1000 c.c. O.H.V. Std. Twin	15°	60°	63°	23°	45°
†175 c.c. O.H.V. Racing	38°	68°	63°	22°	45°
†250 c.c. O.H.V. Racing	24°	55°	62°	25°	45°
350 c.c. O.H.V. Racing (1947-8)					
500 c.c. ,, ,,	45°	65°	70°	35°	42°
500, 350 c.c. Speedway (1947-8)					
*1000 c.c. O.H.V. Racing Twin	25°	66°	65°	23°	45°
†1000 c.c. O.H.V. Racing Twin	15°	60°	63°	23°	45°
*8/75 h.p. Touring	15°	65°	65°	25°	45° 42°L/C
8/80 h.p. Racing (1947-8)	45°	65°	70°	35°	38°H/C

* These timings are applicable to 1935-7 engines only
† These apply to 1932-4 engines

with detachable heads, the position of the piston can be accurately ascertained by removing the cylinder head, although this is not really essential. On all 1927-52 J.A.P. overhead-valve and "high camshaft" engines remove the sparking plug (a compression cock on some side-valve engines can be utilized) and insert either a T.D.C. indicator or a piece of stiff wire or a pencil through the plug hole until it rests on the piston crown, and then rock the crankshaft to and fro until the position of the piston is such that slight rocking produces *no movement* on the part of the indicator or wire. This is the T.D.C. position, and it is now necessary to revolve the engine slowly backwards until the piston is 17 mm. (or whatever the correct spark advance is) below T.D.C. position. To do this where the cylinder head is removed it is only necessary to measure the distance with a small rule. Where the cylinder head is not removed and no calibrated indicator is provided, scratch a mark on the wire or pencil previously mentioned to indicate T.D.C. and make another nick 17 mm. (or whatever is the advance) *above* the T.D.C. mark and rotate the engine *backwards* until the top mark occupies the position of the bottom mark. Obviously the piston will have descended a distance equal to that between the two scratches. This is the correct position of the piston at which the spark should be timed to occur with the ignition control on full advance. Hold this position.

Adjusting the "Break." Next check that the spark control lever or twist-grip is in the fully advanced position (check the action of the control at the magneto) and proceed to remove the contact-breaker cover. Examine the contacts carefully. They should be just beginning to separate if the timing is correct. If it is not, in the case of a Lucas "Magdyno," Lucas "Maglita" or magneto, remove the magneto chain case cover and proceed to loosen the lock-nut on the armature spindle and release the sprocket (without removing the chain) from its taper. If the sprocket is very stiff on the taper, the best plan is to wedge a lever behind it and then tap the lock-nut smartly. If it still refuses to budge, use an extractor tool. The armature can now be revolved slowly by hand until the contacts are beginning to "break." Probably the best and easiest way of checking this is to open the contacts and slip a very thin piece of paper (such as tissue paper) between them. By pulling on the paper while slowly revolving the magneto armature, the commencement of the "break" can be accurately determined. In this position retighten the magneto sprocket lock-nut. When tightening the lock-nut avoid straining the armature spindle in any way and do not hold the spindle by means of the contact-breaker. Finally check over the timing again, check the tension of the magneto chain (where fitted) and refit the timing case cover, not forgetting to use jointing compound or in the case of the "high camshaft" engines a good paper washer to make an oil-tight joint. See also page 74.

On Twin-cylinder Engines. The foregoing instructions apply to Vee twin-cylinder models, but care should be taken to see that No. 1 "break" at the contact-breaker is correct for No. 1 cylinder (firing first) which is at the *rear* on Vee twins. The cams are numbered and, as may be seen in Fig. 30, No. 1 cam which is for the rear (firing) cylinder is the one following the shorter space between the two cams, when considered in the direction of armature rotation. On some Vee Twins the magneto is bevel-driven off the camshaft and in this case when retiming the ignition it is necessary to remove the bevel cap-cover screws and then loosen the locknut securing the bevel on the camshaft and free the bevel from the taper; this permits the armature being turned until the contacts are "breaking" at No. 1 cam with the rear piston the correct distance before T.D.C.

Be careful not to interchange the h.t. leads to the cylinders.

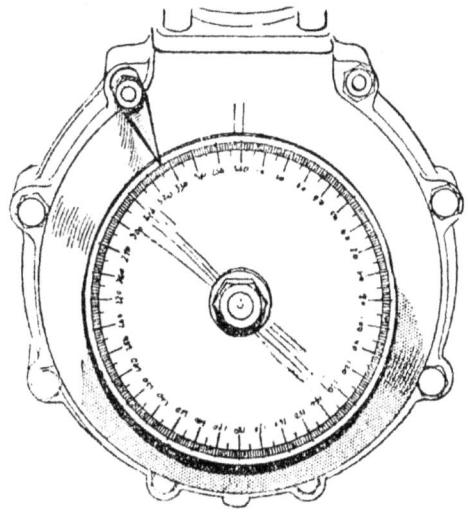

FIG. 32. SHOWING CRANKSHAFT DEGREE DISK FOR VALVE AND IGNITION TIMING

A suitable pointer can be fixed as shown to one of the crankcase bolts. T.D.C position must first be accurately found

(*By courtesy of "The Motor Cycle"*)

On Coil Ignition Models. On coil ignition models with a Lucas or Miller dynamo having the contacts operated by a central cam, it is unnecessary to loosen the driving sprocket on its shaft in order to time the "break," since the cam on the end of the armature spindle can be loosened and turned to the desired position after removing the centre fixing screw. If the cam is stiff, screw a $\frac{5}{16}$ in. bolt into the hole until the cam is pushed off the armature spindle. In some cases a slot is provided on the cam for a hammer and punch. See also page 74.

On 750 c.c. and 1100 c.c. Twins with coil ignition the contact-breaker is housed separately on the timing cover.

Adjusting Magneto Chain. The magneto chain being completely enclosed and automatically lubricated, seldom requires

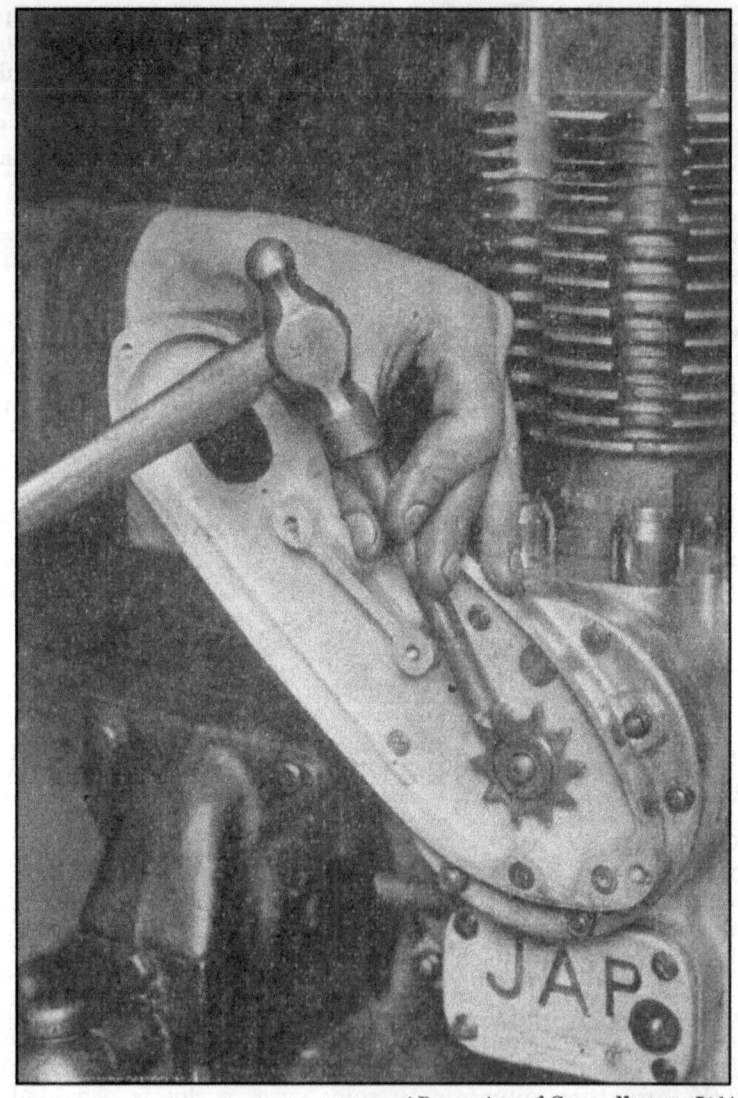

(*By courtesy of George Newnes, Ltd.*)
FIG. 33. REMOVING THE MAGNETO DRIVING SPROCKET PRELIMINARY TO TAKING OFF THE TIMING COVER

ADJUSTMENTS AND OVERHAUL

retensioning, unless, of course, the magneto has been moved on its platform. It is important not to let the chain run too taut because this imposes a severe side strain on the armature spindle. At the centre of the chain run there should be a total deflection of approximately $\tfrac{3}{16}$ in. To retension the chain, loosen the fixing bolts and slide the instrument the necessary amount to the rear. On the 1937-52 "high camshaft" engines the magneto chain is automatically tensioned by means of a spring steel tensioner (see Fig. 17) and no adjustment is needed.

Valve Timing. To the beginner it seems complicated, but it should be borne in mind that an approximate valve timing for all engines is such that the exhaust valve is almost closed and the inlet valve just opening with the piston at top dead centre on the exhaust stroke. To obtain high efficiency, however, an approximate timing will *not* do and the setting arrived at by Messrs. J. A. Prestwich & Co., Ltd., after exhaustive experiments cannot be bettered. These settings are given in the timing charts (see pages 2, 55, 75, 142).

Valve and Ignition Timings (1939-52 500/600 C.C. O.H.V.). The correct timings are identical to those tabulated on page 55 for the 500 c.c. Standard and Sports engines. It should be noted that 40 degrees before T.D.C. on the crankshaft is equivalent to $\tfrac{15}{32}$ in. before T.D.C. on the piston stroke. It should also be observed that on the 500/600 c.c. O.H.V. engines of the type shown in Fig. 34, the camshaft sprocket, *not* the magneto sprocket should be freed and moved relative to its shaft when timing the ignition.

Valve and Ignition Timings ("High Camshaft" Engines). The table on page 55 does not include the "high camshaft" timings. The correct valve timings for 1938 and subsequent "high camshaft" engines are tabulated below.

"HIGH CAMSHAFT" VALVE TIMINGS (1938 ONWARDS)

C.C.	Inlet Opens	Inlet Closes	Exhaust Opens	Exhaust Closes
250	30° before T.D.C.	53° after B.D.C.	71° before B.D.C.	16° after T.D.C.
350	30° before T.D.C.	53° after B.D.C.	71° before B.D.C.	16° after T.D.C.
500	41° before T.D.C.	71° after B.D.C.	75° before B.D.C.	28° after T.D.C.

As regards the ignition timings for 1938 and subsequent "high camshaft" engines, these are as follows: for 250 c.c. and 350 c.c.

engines 40 degrees before T.D.C. on *full advance*; for 500 c.c. engines 36 degrees before T.D.C., also on full advance.

Timing Gears are Punch-marked. To avoid the necessity for retiming the valves after dismantling the timing gear, the gear teeth are marked. A single camwheel is provided on J.A.P. singles but most twin-cylinder engines have two; to ensure that the valves are correctly timed it is only necessary to see that the dot mark on one of the small engine pinion teeth registers with the dot mark between two of the camwheel teeth. If the gears are always replaced in this manner, the timing is bound to be correct, unless the small engine pinion has been removed (see paragraph below). On the "high camshaft" engines a tooth on the driving sprocket is dot-marked and there is also a similar mark between two teeth on the half-time sprocket.

Dismantling J.A.P. Timing Gear. The magneto chain-case cover must first be removed by unscrewing the fixing screws and the next step is to remove the magneto driving sprocket from the camshaft extension with a sprocket drawer after unscrewing the lock-nut. If no drawer is available, tap the sprocket at the roots of the teeth with a brass punch and hammer as shown in Fig. 33. The sprocket is *not* keyed and a smart blow should release the sprocket from the taper on the camshaft. Remove both sprockets.

Having removed the magneto sprocket, now undo the ¼ in. nuts from the timing case cover and the screw inside the chain case; the cover should then be gently tapped off. Keep pressure against the camwheel so as to prevent its coming away before the timing marks have been checked. The valve lifter cam may be combined on the lifter pin and, if the lifter pin rod is worked up and down, this will readily free itself. Remove the camwheel, rotary valve, and the cam followers.

Where the Magneto is Bevel-driven. On Vee Twins having a bevel-driven magneto, before the timing cover can be removed it is necessary to remove the bevel from the camshaft. To do this, remove the three bevel cap-cover screws, take the magneto off its base, and with a box spanner remove the bevel locking nut. The bevel may then be freed from the camshaft taper with a brass punch and hammer, as in the case of the magneto sprocket.

If the Engine Pinion is Removed. During a thorough overhaul it is sometimes necessary to remove the small engine pinion from the tapered and keyed mainshaft with the aid of an extractor tool after undoing the lock-nut (L.H. thread) with a box spanner and long tommy-bar. If this is done, careful note should be taken as to the method of keying the pinion to the main shaft. As a rule, there are three key-ways provided on the pinion, but on some engines five key-ways are cut on the vernier system so as to enable the valve timing to be varied by one-fifth of a tooth. If this is the case, to avoid upsetting the original timing, it is essential to use the correct key-way on reassembly, and it should therefore be marked during dismantling. If there is any doubt as to which is the correct key-way, it is advisable to retime the valves according to the maker's setting (see chart on page 55).

To Retime the Valves. If there is any doubt as to the accuracy of the valve timing, it should be checked and the valves if necessary retimed. The points to check are (a) the opening of the inlet valve, and (b) the closing of the exhaust valve. If these two points are accurately determined, obviously the closing of the inlet valve and the opening of the exhaust valve must *necessarily* be correct also, for the cam contours see to this automatically. Where a single camwheel is fitted, it is obviously only necessary to time the correct opening of the inlet valve.

As in the case of timing the ignition (page 54), two methods are available for setting the advance before T.D.C. for the opening of the inlet valve and the retard after T.D.C. for the closing of the exhaust valve. Measurements can either be taken on the piston stroke, or else a degree disk can be attached to the crankshaft (Fig. 32), and the crank positions relatively to T.D.C. determined according to the J.A.P. timing chart (see also page 59).

If a degree disk is attached to the crankshaft (and this method is preferable owing to the great accuracy provided and needed), the first step is to locate the exact position of T.D.C. With the piston stroke method this can be done as described on page 54. The next step (and this is very important) is to *adjust the valve clearances correctly*, otherwise the valves will open earlier or later than they should do. It should be particularly noted that *normal* valve clearances are suitable for valve timing purposes on J.A.P. engines. The camwheel should be meshed with the engine pinion in several positions until the correct advance and retard in millimetres or degrees before and after T.D.C. for the inlet and exhaust valves respectively is obtained. Timing of the valves must be done on the *exhaust stroke*, and not the compression stroke as in ignition timing. On all engines there is a valve overlap (i.e. the inlet opens before the exhaust closes) and a rough check on the timing is to "rock" the engine sprocket to and fro either side of T.D.C. position on the exhaust stroke, when the inlet valve should open and the exhaust valve close in quick succession. Always time the inlet valve first and the exhaust valve afterwards. When refitting the timing case cover, do not forget to replace the paper washer for the joint on "high camshaft" engines. On other engines use a jointing compound.

If the Timing Gears are Worn. When an engine begins to get old, considerable wear on the teeth of the timing gears may be present (which would be indicated by noise), and if it is not

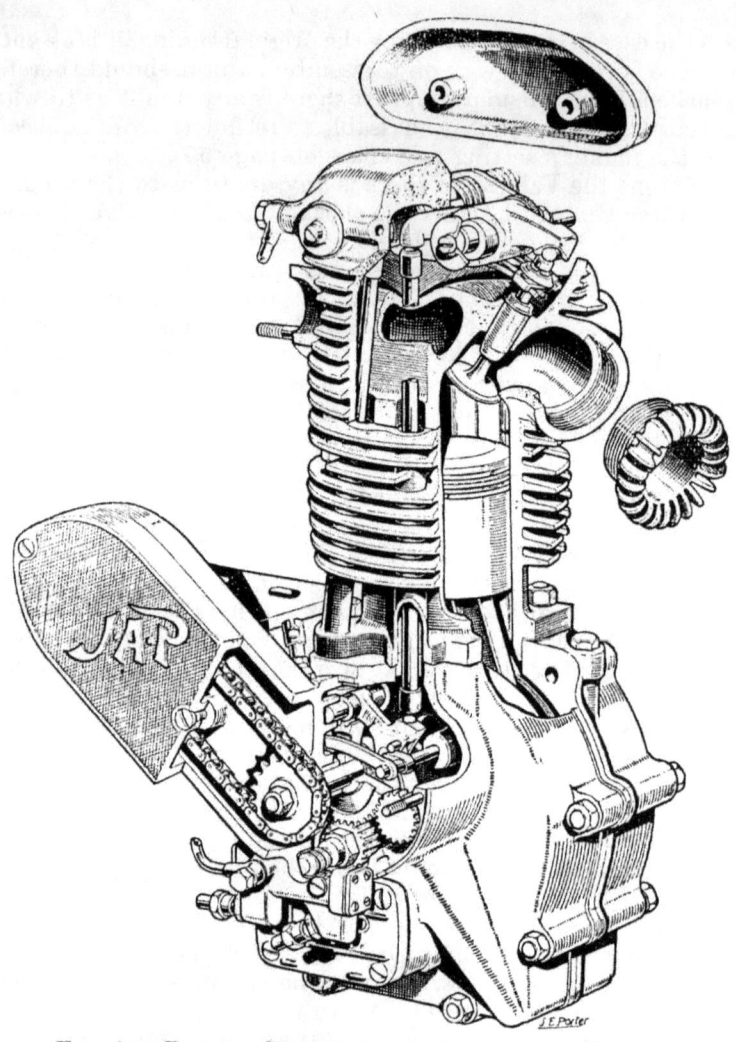

Fig. 34. Partly Sectioned and cut-away View of 1939–52 500/600 c.c. O.H.V. J.A.P. Engine

A prominent feature of this engine, which has a compression ratio of 5·4 to 1, is the very thorough valve enclosure. The big-end has a double row roller bearing, and both main shafts have roller bearings. The timing gear has a single camwheel with twin cams, and the push-rods rest directly on roller type cam followers. The correct valve and ignition timings for this engine are the same as given in the chart on page 55 for the 500 c.c. Standard and Sports engines. Note that 40 degrees is equivalent to 15/32 in. before T.D.C. Follow the instructions on pages 53–63, but observe that the *camshaft* sprocket, not the magneto sprocket, should be freed and moved on its shaft

(*By courtesy of* " *Motor Cycling* ")

ADJUSTMENTS AND OVERHAUL

considered worth while fitting new gears, some improvement in engine performance can sometimes be obtained by using an alternative key-way.

WEAR OF CYLINDER PISTON, ETC.

Inspecting Cylinder. To examine for vertical scratches or scoring hold the cylinder so that light passes down the bore. If there is only slight scoring present, this can usually be remedied by lapping-in an old piston, but if the scoring is deep it is necessary to have the cylinder reground and a new piston and rings fitted by the makers, or else to have the scores built up by a special type of welding process. Regrinding and the fitting of an oversize piston and rings are also required if the cylinder bore has become worn badly and is oval where the rings travel. Measurements of the cylinder diameter may be taken with a pair of internal callipers at various points in the bore with which the callipers must be kept quite square. On new engines of 70 mm. bore the piston clearance is 0·004 in. to 0·006 in. at the bottom of the skirt and the taper is 0·002 in. per inch of skirt length. After a big mileage has been covered the cylinder bore tends to become oval. Little wear occurs at the extreme top and bottom but a distinct ridge usually forms at the top position of the upper piston ring where wear is greatest due to connecting-rod thrust. From this point wear gradually decreases to the bottom position of the lowest ring. With a cast-iron cylinder of 70-80 mm. bore and light alloy piston, if cylinder wear exceeds 0·005 in. a new cylinder and piston, or a rebore, are required. It should be noted that where considerable cylinder ovality exists it is useless to fit new rings only as they are bound to make poor circumferential contact.

The Piston Rings. As the rings are responsible for maintaining engine compression they must make good circumferential contact with the cylinder walls, be free but good fits in the piston grooves, and have the correct size gaps between the ends. The rings must also be springy and exert uniform pressure.

A simple method of testing for circumferential contact is to push a ring into and square with the cylinder bore and hold it in front of a source of light. If contact is bad, rays will penetrate between the ring and cylinder and it will be possible to slip a 0·001 in.–0·002 in. feeler gauge between the two.

New J.A.P. piston rings have a side play in the piston ring grooves of 0·0035 in.–0·005 in. for rings of $\frac{3}{32}$ in. width, and 0·0025 in.–0·004 in. for rings of $\frac{1}{16}$ in. width. If excessive play of the rings (0·004 in.–0·006 in.) develops, fit new rings, or if the ring grooves are worn fit a new piston. Oversize width rings are not available. To test a ring for side play, place it in its groove and note how much it can be moved up and down. Another method is to remove the ring and roll it around the groove.

As has already been mentioned on page 24, a fair average gap for piston rings on J.A.P. engines is for standard engines 0·003 in. per inch of bore diameter and for racing engines 0·005 in. If the gap exceeds 0·020 in. on standard engines, new rings are needed. If new rings are fitted, it is essential to see that the gaps are not too small, otherwise an engine seizure may be caused. To increase the gap, clamp the ring in a vice (using soft clams) and carefully file the ends. The best method of testing the gap is to push a ring up into the cylinder with the piston skirt a short distance and then check the gap with a feeler gauge of the right thickness. If an engine has been dismantled, examine the ends of the rings and note if they are carbonized or polished; if polished, the gap is probably too small. If new rings are a tight fit in their grooves, rub the rings on one side on a sheet of carborundum paper laid on a piece of plate glass.

Testing Mainshaft Bearings. Although 0·015 in. to 0·020 in. crankshaft end play is permissible, there should be no appreciable "shake" in the roller bearings (a bronze bearing is sometimes used on the timing side). To test for "shake," grip the engine sprocket with both hands and try to "rock" the crankshaft. If the timing cover has been removed, see if it is possible to lever up the timing side mainshaft slightly with a tyre lever. End play of the crankshaft can be taken up by fitting new thrust washers.

Testing for Play in Big-end Bearing. Disperse the oil film on the big-end bearing with some paraffin and then after putting the connecting-rod at T.D.C. or B.D.C. try to push and pull the rod vertically, when any appreciable play in the roller big-end should be at once felt. If much play exists, a new roller bearing should be fitted and as this necessitates parting the flywheels (a delicate operation requiring much care in subsequent truing up) and pressing a new race into the big-end, it is best to return the complete crankcase and flywheel assembly to Messrs. J. A. Prestwich & Co., Ltd., for expert attention (address page 139) A sectional view of the big-end assembly provided on 1100 c.c. Vee-twin J.A.P. engines is shown on page 140.

Note Concerning O.H.V. Valve Guides. On most single-cylinder O.H.V. engines inlet and exhaust valve guides are *not* interchangeable. The guide for the inlet valve is of steel, while that for the exhaust valve is of steel with a *bronze liner*.

J.A.P. Racing Engines. All previously given maintenance instructions apply to most J.A.P. racing engines, but note the advice given on page 141.

CHAPTER IV
THE S.V. VERTICAL TWIN J.A.P.

As has been mentioned in the Preface, a J.A.P. power unit, entirely different in design from other J.A.P. engines, has been produced and fitted to an attractive A.J.W. motor-cycle, a brief description of which is given in Chapter VIII. In this chapter the author has included an outline of the interesting S.V. engine and some helpful instructions concerning its general maintenance.

OUTLINE OF S.V. ENGINE

The S.V. engine has a bore and stroke of 63·5 mm. × 78 mm., giving a capacity of 494 c.c. Figs. 35 and 36 show details of the engine, which is silent, has O.H.V. acceleration, and gives a top speed of about 75 m.p.h. Maximum revs. are 4800 r.p.m.

Crankshaft and Connecting-rod Assembly. The crankshaft is a one-piece forging with two counter-weights and bolted-on central flywheel. The main shafts run in large single-row ball and roller bearings. Other features include: $1\frac{1}{2}$ in. diameter crank-pins; connecting rods with split big-ends having renewable shells; small-ends with bronze bushes and fully floating gudgeon-pins. Each light alloy piston has two compression rings and one oil control ring.

Cylinder Block and Head. The truncated monobloc type cylinder head has air passages between the cylinders and around the exhaust ports to ensure good cooling. The valves are inclined at 4 degrees to the vertical, have duplex springs and tappets housed in accessible chests. The inlet port is between the exhaust ports, and the flange-fitted carburettor is of the Amal needle-jet type. The detachable one-piece aluminium alloy cylinder head gives a C.R. of 6 to 1, has an aluminium gasket, and long-reach 14 mm. plugs.

The Camshaft. The camshaft is driven from the engine main shaft by a chain which runs in an oil bath. It runs in "Oilite" bushes and the cams actuate the flat-base tappets direct. Provision for tappet clearances is in the form of shims inserted beneath the tappet end caps. A spring-loaded blade automatically tensions the driving chain.

Ignition and Lighting. Current for coil ignition and lighting is supplied by a special Lucas dynamo driven by separate chain from the engine shaft. A reduction gear for the contact-breaker is incorporated and the automatic ignition advance mechanism is of the centrifugal type.

66   THE BOOK OF THE J.A.P.

Lubrication System. This is of the "dipper" type, the sump being integral with the crankcase. Below each big-end is a light alloy trough and the hollow "dipper" stalk on each connecting-rod cap dips into the elevated trough, thereby forcing oil to the

(*By courtesy of "Motor Cycling"*)

FIG. 35. SIMPLICITY AND NEATNESS—THE 494 c.c. S.V. VERTICAL TWIN J.A.P. ENGINE

The strangler device on the carburettor shown is replaced on most motor-cycles by normal two-lever handlebar operated control

bearings and splash lubricating the camshaft, pistons and cylinder bores. Surplus oil drains to the sump above whose base the troughs are raised. Four disk-type pressure release valves behind the camshaft sprocket are responsible for lubrication of the timing gear and the chain which runs in an oil bath.

THE S.V. VERTICAL TWIN J.A.P.

Exploded View of Engine. An excellent exploded view of the S.V. vertical twin engine is reproduced on page 71 by kind permission of *Motor Cycling*. On the engine illustrated a single triangular-shaped chain drives both the camshaft and the dyno-distributor unit, and a spring-loaded steel blade and a fibre block are used for automatically tensioning the chain. It should be noted that this arrangement was used on *development* engines only. On all production engines the large sprocket on the camshaft is driven by a $\frac{3}{8}$ in. pitch chain from the engine main-shaft sprocket. A second duplex sprocket is fitted to the main shaft and the dyno-distributor unit is driven from this sprocket by a separate 8 mm. duplex chain running in front of the camshaft driving chain. The fibre block is omitted.

Both main shaft sprockets are keyed, and the camshaft sprocket has three key-ways to enable the timing to be varied within one-third of a tooth (to compensate for wear). On later type engines the camshaft drive sprocket (on the engine main shaft) incorporates vernier timing.

GENERAL MAINTENANCE

Recommended Engine Oils. The engine manufacturers recommend the replenishment of the oil sump with one of the following brands and grades of engine oils—

(1) Castrol XXL (Castrol XL in winter).
(2) Mobiloil BB (Mobiloil A in winter).
(3) Shell X-100 SAE 50 (Shell X-100 SAE 40 in winter).
(4) Essolube 50 (Essolube 30 in winter).
(5) Price's Energol SAE 40 (SAE 30 in winter).

Replenishing the Oil Sump. The combined filler cap and dipstick should be removed often from the neck on the off-side of the oil sump, and the oil level inspected and the tank if necessary topped up with one of the above-mentioned engine oils.

To check the level of oil in the sump, unscrew the filler cap, wipe the dip-stick with a clean rag, and then *rest* the filler cap on the neck protruding from the sump. After a few seconds withdraw the filler cap and carefully inspect the position of the top edge of the oil film adhering to the dip-stick. Only by adopting this procedure can the true level of oil in the sump be determined. Unscrewing the filler cap and immediately examining the dipstick will indicate a higher level of oil than is actually the case.

The dip-stick has two marks, "H" and "L," indicating high and low oil levels, and it is important that the level should not be allowed to rise above the "H" mark or fall below the "L" mark. For preference, the level should be maintained at, or slightly above, the mid-way position.

Because the oil troughs are raised above the crankcase base, the lubrication system incorporates no filter. For this reason it is advisable to replenish the sump with *filtered* oil if the purity of the oil being used for replenishment is in the slightest degree doubtful. When replenishing from sealed cans, this question does not, of course, arise.

Maintenance of Lubrication System. Owing to simplicity of design, the lubrication system requires practically no maintenance other than regular replenishment of the oil sump, referred to above, and its occasional draining and cleaning. All sludge and impurities which accumulate during running fall to the base of the sump, which should be thoroughly cleaned when decarbonizing, i.e. about every 3000 miles.

To clean the oil sump, it is advisable to flush out the crankcase with a thin oil. Alternatively use a proprietary flushing oil. After thorough cleaning and draining has been completed, see that the drain plug is firmly retightened and replenish the sump with one of the previously mentioned engine oils.

Lubrication of Dyno-distributor. The Lucas dyno-distributor unit is packed with grease by the makers on assembly, and no further lubrication of the bearings should be needed until a very big mileage has been covered, when the instrument should be returned to the makers for cleaning, general overhaul and greasing. Occasionally add a spot of oil to the felt disk responsible for lubricating the contact-breaker cam, but beware of excessive lubrication here, otherwise there is a risk of oil finding its way on to the contacts and causing much bother.

Suitable Sparking Plugs. Messrs. J. A. Prestwich & Co., Ltd. recommend a 14 mm., long reach, Lodge CLN or CB14, or a Champion L-10S sparking plug. If it is desired to use a K.L.G. plug, a suitable type is the 14 mm., long reach, K.L.G. F.50. Maintain the gap between the centre and outer electrodes at 0.020 in. -0.022 in., and keep the two plugs thoroughly clean. Some advice on cleaning plugs will be found on pages 47 and 52.

The Contact-breaker. The gap between the contacts of the Lucas contact-breaker, used for the coil ignition, should be maintained at 0.018 in. to 0.020 in. Remove the cover and inspect the contact-breaker about every 1000-1500 miles. If the contacts are in need of adjustment, as indicated by a feeler gauge, this can readily be effected by loosening the two screws which secure the plate carrying the fixed contact, and swivelling the plate slightly as required. One of the two screws passes through a slot which limits the movement of the plate. If the contacts are dirty or pitted, clean them up. Some useful hints on cleaning the contacts are given on page 51. After making the adjustment, tighten the two screws firmly.

THE S.V. VERTICAL TWIN J.A.P.

Carburettor Tuning and Maintenance. The carburettor, which is flange-fitted to the *front* of the cylinder block between the two exhaust ports, is a vertical two-lever Amal (type 276/004R 39A). It has a needle-type main jet and a pilot jet, and is almost identical to the carburettor (see Fig. 23) used on the other J.A.P. engines. Handlebar control is provided for both the throttle and air slides. On some vertical twin carburettors, however, an Amal air filter (type 96/101) is used on the air intake. The filter embodies a fine gauze element which requires no attention except cleaning with petrol at long intervals.

Carburettor tuning and maintenance instructions are exactly the same as for the instrument fitted to the other engines (see pages 41–4). The usual carburettor setting is to use a $\frac{15}{16}$ in. choke in conjunction with a size 140 main jet, 6/3 throttle valve, and a middle needle position. See also page 92.

Starting the Vertical Twin. On motor-cycles fitted with the S.V. vertical twin engine the ignition lever and the exhaust valve lifter are omitted. To set the controls for starting it is only necessary to open the throttle about one-eighth and close the air lever completely. If the engine is already warm, the air lever should be opened slightly. Starting is not critical in any way, and if the engine fails to respond to the second kick, a slightly larger throttle opening should be used. Avoid excessive flooding of the carburettor. As soon as the engine starts, open the air lever fully. The automatic ignition-advance mechanism sees to it that the spark is automatically advanced with increase of engine revolutions and the ignition question can be forgotten.

Be Careful During the First 1500 Miles. A few motor-cycle manufacturers (e.g. Cotton) run their engines in prior to delivery, but the majority do not. If you desire to obtain maximum performance from your vertical twin for the longest possible time, it is *essential* to drive very carefully during the first 1000 miles. See that the oil level in the sump is properly maintained, and use the controls with discretion. Avoid large throttle openings and make the fullest use of the gearbox. On no account indulge in sudden bursts of speed or allow the engine to labour and become overheated. Half to three-quarter throttle is the most which should be used, even during the last stage of running-in.

Failure to run-in a new J.A.P. engine properly often results in the engine being *permanently* spoiled. The cylinder bores and all bearing surfaces of a new engine *appear* to be dead smooth, but actually they are covered with fine tool marks which easily cause friction. With careful running-in, all surfaces gradually assume a mirror-like gloss and hardness. See also page 90.

Adjusting the Tappets. The correct tappet clearance is the same as on the other J.A.P. side-valve engines, namely 0·004 in.

for the inlet valve and 0·006 in. for the exhaust valve, with the engine *cold*. The tappet clearances should be checked every few thousand miles, but actual adjustment is needed under normal conditions only about every 4000-6000 miles.

To check the tappet clearances, first remove the pressed-steel cover plates from the two valve chests after unscrewing the two bolts. This exposes the stems of the four $\frac{5}{16}$ in. diameter valves (inclined at 4 degrees to the vertical), the duplex valve springs, and the four tappets. Then insert a suitable feeler gauge between each tappet cap and the corresponding valve, after first making sure that both valves of the cylinder concerned are fully closed with the piston at T.D.C. on the compression stroke.

If the clearance of a tappet is found to be incorrect, lift the valve with the special J.A.P. tool provided, and with the J.A.P. tappet cap removal tool remove the tappet cap. Then grease and fit a suitable shim between the end cap and tappet head as required. Several alternative shims are available. These shims have a thickness of 0·003 in., 0·005 in., and 0·010 in. Having fitted the shim required to obtain the correct tappet clearance, replace the tappet cap (a sliding fit) on the hollow flat-base tappet, and again check the clearance.

Check and if necessary adjust all four tappet-clearances as described above, replace the valve chest covers and tighten the two cover securing bolts. If the engine is running well, the tappet adjustment should not be interfered with.

Decarbonize About Every 3000 Miles. Under normal conditions of running it should not be necessary to decarbonize more often than about every 3000 miles, except in the case of a new engine where decarbonizing is advisable after the first 2000 miles.

To decarbonize it is only necessary to remove the cylinder head, but if there is poor compression it is advisable to remove the cylinder block also, so that the condition of the pistons, piston rings and valves can be examined. If loss of compression is due to pitting of the valves and/or valve seats, the valves must be ground-in. The engine manufacturers, however, recommend that the cylinder block itself be removed as least often as possible if compression remains good. When perusing the following stripping down and assembly instructions, reference should be made to Fig. 36, which shows an exploded view of the side-valve engine.

Removing Cylinder Head. It is generally unnecessary to remove the petrol tank if it is intended to remove the cylinder head only. But if it is intended to remove the cylinder block also, petrol tank removal greatly facilitates stripping down of the engine.

To remove the cylinder head, first disconnect the h.t. leads from both sparking plugs. Then unscrew evenly and in a diagonal

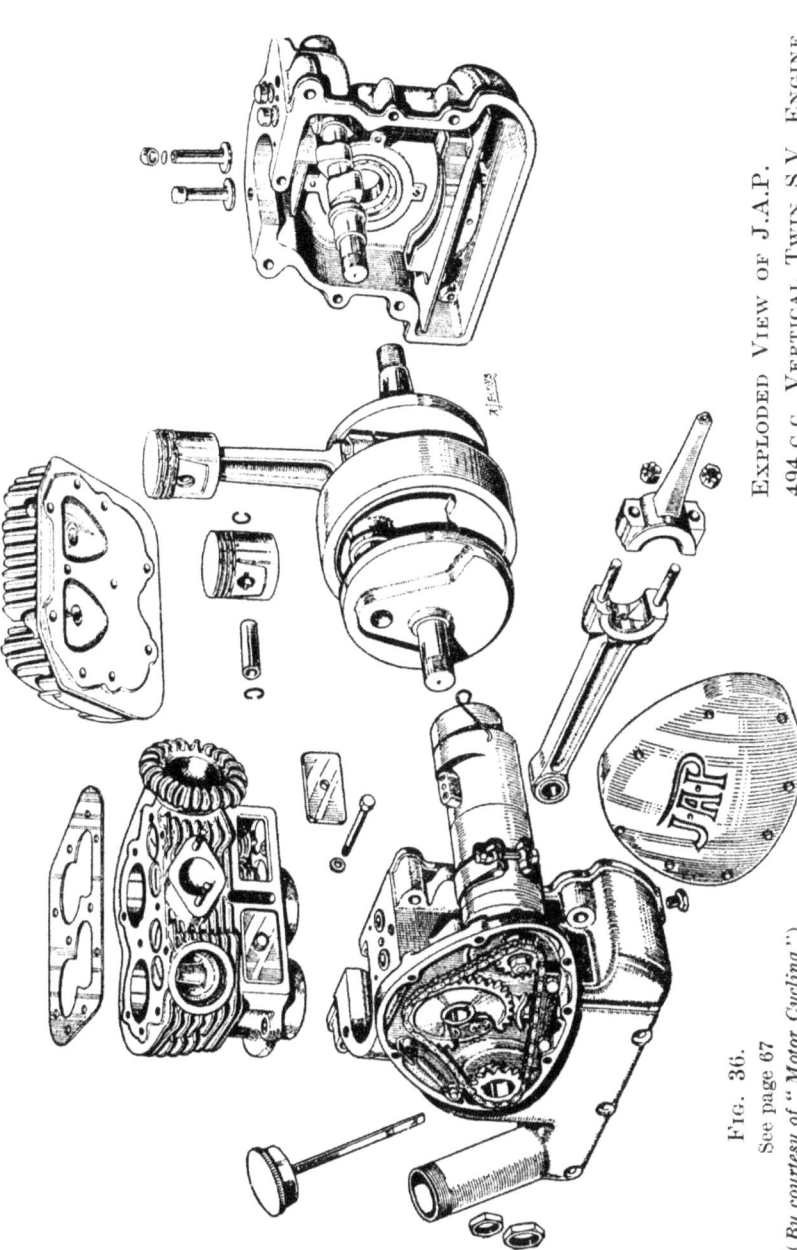

Fig. 36.
See page 67
(*By courtesy of "Motor Cycling"*)

Exploded View of J.A.P.
494 c.c. Vertical Twin S.V. Engine

order the ten $\frac{5}{16}$ in. cylinder head securing bolts, and remove them. Now lift the cylinder head off the cylinder block, and also the plain *aluminium* gasket interposed between the two. If the cylinder head joint is stiff, tap the head gently near the exhaust ports, but do not attempt to prise it off, otherwise the soft metal gasket may be damaged. Inspect the gasket carefully and note whether there is any evidence of "blowing."

Removing Cylinder Block. Having removed the petrol tank, cylinder head, and gasket, proceed to remove both exhaust pipes by unscrewing the finned ring nuts securing them to the two ports. Then disconnect the feed pipe to the Amal carburettor, unscrew the mixing chamber cap, withdraw the throttle and air slides, and remove the carburettor from the flange at the front of the cylinder block. Be careful not to damage the cooperite joint washer.

Now remove the covers from both valve chests by unscrewing the two securing bolts. Having done this, unscrew evenly and in a diagonal order the six nuts securing the cylinder block to the crankcase. Four of these nuts are external, and one nut is located *inside* each valve chest. The one-piece cast-iron cylinder block can now be gently eased off the two pistons, which should be placed near B.D.C. before the block is withdrawn. Both hands should be used to remove the block and it is therefore advisable to obtain assistance so as to avoid the possibility of imposing any side strain or allowing the freed pistons to fall sharply against the mouth of the crankcase. Cover up the hole immediately with a clean rag to prevent the entry of dirt, tappet caps, etc.

Piston Removal. To remove each light alloy piston it is only necessary to remove *one* circlip (with a pair of round-nosed pliers) and then push the hollow fully-floating gudgeon-pin out from the opposite side. After removal, each piston should be marked (see page 21), if this has not already been done, so as to ensure correct replacement in the correct cylinder bore. No identification marks are provided by the manufacturers. It is not necessary to renew the gudgeon-pin circlip each time the piston is removed, unless the old one has been damaged during removal.

Removing, Cleaning, and Refitting Piston Rings. The instructions given on pages 21–4 are applicable and should be carefully noted. On the J.A.P. vertical twin the correct piston ring gap for the two compression rings and the oil control ring is 0·008 in. to 0·010 in. for *new* rings. As on the other types of J.A.P. engines, the maximum permissible worn gap is 0·020 in. On new pistons, the correct clearance between the piston rings and the grooves in which they fit is 0·001 in. to 0·003 in. It should be noted that the oil control ring is *not* a scraper ring and may be refitted either way round.

Scraping Off Carbon Deposits. Follow the general instructions given on pages 24-5, but where decarbonizing is undertaken with the cylinder block not removed, do *not* use any kind of abrasive on the piston crowns. If such abrasive should get between the pistons and cylinder bores, a ruined cylinder block is not only likely, but probable.

Grinding-in the Valves. While it is possible to grind-in the valves with the cylinder block in position on the engine, it is much more satisfactory and convenient to do this with the cylinder block removed. To remove the valves, compress each duplex valve spring with the J.A.P. valve spring compressor and then extract the split collet and withdraw the valve, valve spring, and spring collars. Be careful not to interchange any of the four valves, as they are ground individually on to their seats and are not marked by the makers for identification.

Check the valve guides for wear and proceed to grind-in each valve as described on pages 28-9, if the valve and/or seat is pitted. The heads of all four valves are slotted to take a screwdriver or the bit of a hand brace. After grinding-in each valve, make absolutely certain that all traces of grinding paste are removed. Having ground-in the valves, replace them in their original seats and assemble the valve springs as described on page 29. Afterwards replace the valve chest covers, but do not tighten their securing bolts firmly as the covers must be removed prior to tightening down the cylinder block.

Engine Assembly. Replace the pistons and cylinder block in the reverse order of dismantling. The advice given on page 30 is generally applicable, but certain points should be noted. See that a new oil-resisting paper washer is fitted to the base of the cylinder block, and use jointing compound to attach the washer to the cylinder block face only. Check that all four tappet end caps, shims, and tappet heads are in position on the tappets. When easing the block over the pistons, obtain assistance to keep the pistons square with the bores and to facilitate entry of the piston rings. Be sure to tighten down the cylinder block securing nuts evenly and diagonally, and do not forget the nut located inside each valve chest in addition to the four external nuts.

Replace the aluminium cylinder head gasket and then fit the cylinder head. Replace the two *centre* bolts first and tighten all ten securing bolts evenly and firmly, in a diagonal order, so as to relieve strain. Finally replace in this order: the carburettor, petrol pipe, both exhaust pipes, both sparking plugs and h.t. leads, and lastly the petrol tank, if this has been removed. If the valves have been ground-in, check over the valve clearances. Also after completing a short mileage, check over all nuts and bolts for tightness.

Timing the Ignition. The chain-driven Lucas dyno-distributor unit supplies current for the coil ignition system and the lighting system. The dynamo itself runs slightly faster than the engine, but the reduction gear incorporated reduces the speed of the contact-breaker to *half engine speed*. As has been previously mentioned, automatic ignition advance mechanism (of the centrifugal type) is included, so that once the timing is correctly set, no attention to the ignition is needed either when starting up or driving. The rotor arm of the distributor moves slightly relative to the cam as the engine speed varies, and thereby automatically advances or retards ignition. Timing the ignition does not in itself involve disturbing the dyno-distributor drive referred to on page 75.

If the ignition timing has been disturbed by removal of the dyno-distributor unit, or by removing its chain drive, accurate re-timing can be very readily effected. The automatic ignition advance mechanism fully retards the ignition when the engine is stationary, and the ignition timing is correct when the contacts of the contact-breaker are beginning to open with the piston at T.D.C. on *full retard*. It is permissible to time on either cylinder, but it is most convenient to time on the cylinder nearest the *timing side* of the engine. This cylinder is generally regarded as No. 1 cylinder.

The procedure for retiming the ignition is as follows. If the sprockets and chain used for driving the dyno-distributor unit have been removed, replace both sprockets and the chain. The sprocket for the engine main shaft is keyed, but that for the dynamo shaft is a taper fit only. Tension the chain so that there is a whip of approximately ⅜ in. at the centre. At this stage the timing case cover can be screwed home if desired.

With the dyno-distributor drive fitted, and chain tension correct, remove the contact-breaker cover. Next loosen the screw located below the contact-breaker spring.

Turn engine till No. 1 piston is at true T.D.C. on the compression stroke (page 54). Verify that it is on the compression stroke by removing the off-side valve chest cover and checking that both valves are closed. It should be observed that on the vertical twin J.A.P. engine one piston is at T.D.C. on the compression stroke and the other piston is at T.D.C. on the exhaust stroke.

Keeping No. 1 piston at T.D.C. on the compression stroke, turn the contact-breaker cam until the contacts are just beginning to open,* and then retighten the screw below the contact-breaker spring. The ignition timing should now be correctly set and the

---

* To ensure that the contacts are beginning to open, lightly pull on a small piece of cigarette paper, or thin tissue paper, inserted between the two contacts.

contact-breaker cover itself can be replaced. Also replace the valve chest cover belonging to No. 1 cylinder. If the h.t. lead for No. 1 plug has been disconnected, reconnect this lead. Note: centre lead conects to coil, and the remaining lead to C.B. on coil.

The h.t. leads have no identification marks, but the *outside* lead is generally taken to the sparking plug of No. 1 cylinder. If both h.t. leads have been disconnected, it is necessary to check that the lead from the distributor segment involved in the retiming is connected to the appropriate sparking plug, otherwise the spark will occur with the piston at T.D.C. on the exhaust stroke instead of the compression stroke!

Retensioning Dyno-distributor Driving Chain. The driving chain has no automatic tensioning device as is used for the camshaft driving chain. It is therefore necessary at occasional intervals to check the tension of the driving chain by removing the timing case cover and inspecting the amount of chain whip present. This should not exceed about ⅜ in. at the centre of the chain. To remedy excessive chain whip, slacken the dynamo securing strap and turn the body of the instrument slightly as required. The dynamo sprocket is eccentric to the body of the instrument in order to provide this means of retensioning the chain. Be very careful not to tighten the driving chain excessively, as this subjects the armature shaft and bearings to stresses for which they are not designed. As regards lubrication of the driving chain, this is an oil-bath supplemented by oil from the crankcase release.

Valve Timing. The arrangement of the automatically tensioned chain drive for the camshaft is referred to on page 67, and it will be noted that the large camshaft has *three* key-ways provided (except on later twins, see page 76, with vernier timing) to

VALVE TIMING FOR S.V. VERTICAL TWIN J.A.P.
ENGINE (1948 ONWARDS)

Inlet Opens	Inlet Closes	Exhaust Opens	Exhaust Closes
18° before T.D.C.	56° after B.D.C.	56° before B.D.C.	15° after T.D.C.

enable the timing to be varied within one-third of a tooth. The rider seldom has occasion to make this precise adjustment, as a simple method of replacing the drive without upsetting the timing is provided for. The maker's valve timing is tabulated above and no attempt should be made to improve upon this timing which has been determined after much calculation and thorough testing.

It should be noted that an extractor tool is provided in order to remove the dyno-distributor driving sprocket, but not the camshaft driving sprocket from the timing side main shaft. Both sprockets are keyed. If the separate drive for the camshaft has been removed, it is possible to replace the drive without upsetting the valve timing by using the following procedure.

Position the piston in No. 1 (the off-side) cylinder at 56 degrees before B.D.C. on the *firing* stroke. This is equivalent to $2\frac{1}{2}$ in. from T.D.C. measured on the piston stroke. Actually retiming can be done on either cylinder, but No. 1 is as convenient as any. Now turn the camshaft slowly *clockwise* until the exhaust valve is just beginning to open. At this point all tappet clearance is taken up and the tappet is just starting to raise the exhaust valve from its seat. Then slide the main shaft sprocket and the large camshaft sprocket on to their respective shafts, together with the driving chain, and with the key-ways of both sprockets *in line* with each other.

After replacing the camshaft it is advisable again to verify the valve timing by checking that the exhaust valve is about to open with the piston $2\frac{1}{2}$ in. from T.D.C. on the firing stroke. Next replace the dyno-distributor chain drive, check the chain tension, and retime the ignition as described on page 74. Finally replace the timing-case cover and screw it home evenly and firmly. Make sure that the timing case gasket is in perfect condition, otherwise oil leakage will probably occur.

Vernier Adjustment for Valve Timing. On all later type S.V. vertical twin J.A.P. engines a simple design of vernier adjustment for the valve timing is provided. A steel pin, which is threaded, is driven into the inner end of the boss of the (outer) duplex sprocket for the dyno-distributor unit driving chain. The (inner) sprocket for the camshaft driving chain is threaded on to the steel pin.

Behind the (inner) sprocket for the camshaft drive is threaded a boss which has a key-way engaging the key on the timing side engine main shaft. This boss has a series of holes adjacent to another series of holes in the sprocket for the camshaft drive. All the holes are on the pitch radius and one series contains *one extra hole*. Thus by turning the boss relative to the camshaft driving sprocket so that a pair of opposite holes coincide it is possible to obtain a vernier adjustment of the position of the camshaft driving sprocket relative to the key on the timing side engine main shaft.

CHAPTER V

HINTS FOR 1934-9 A.J.W. OWNERS

THE hints in this chapter deal with the popular 1934 to 1939 A.J.W. "Red Foxes" and "Flying Foxes,"* but it should be noted that much of the information (except in regard to the engine) applies also to the "Flying Vixen." On this particular model, however, a "Python" engine was fitted in 1934, a special "T.T. Replica" J.A.P. engine in 1935, and a Stevens engine in 1936. It is not possible in this handbook to deal with these engines nor with the two "Lynx" two-strokes.

"Fox" Engine Lubrication. All 1935 and subsequent "Flying Foxes" and all "Red Foxes" of 1934 and later date have a 490 c.c. standard J.A.P. engine with dry sump lubrication. For maintenance instructions the reader is referred to pages 1 to 8. In the case of the 1934 "Flying Fox" a "Python" engine was installed. On all "Foxes" it is important to keep the oil-level at or above the half-full mark in the welded steel separate tank which holds ½ gal. and has a removable gauze filter below the filler cap where the oil return can be observed. Always replenish with one of the engine oils mentioned on page 1 and do not forget to go steady with a new or reconditioned engine during the first 800-1000 miles (see page 69). No adjustment for the oil supply is provided.

Magneto and Dynamo Lubrication. Lucas magnetos and belt-driven Miller dynamos are standard "Fox" equipment (except on 1934 "Red Foxes" which have coil ignition) and advice on lubrication will be found on page 12. When lubricating the Miller dynamo be careful to avoid excessive lubrication, otherwise oil may reach the commutator and cause much trouble.

The A.J.W. Control Layout. The layout of the handlebar controls is as follows. On the left-hand side of the bars there are the ignition lever, the exhaust valve lifter, and the clutch; on the right-hand side are situated the throttle twist-grip, the air lever and the front brake lever. The lighting switch and ammeter are incorporated on the headlamp.

Positive-stop foot gear change is provided on the "Flying Foxes" but not on the "Red Foxes" which have hand control, upward gear changes with foot control being made by depressing the pedal (fully down). The pedal returns to the *same* position

---

* A.J.W. motor-cycles were made by A.J.W. Motor Cycles, Ltd., of Mill Lane, Wimborne, Dorset, but this firm no longer exists. A.J.W. spares and service are, however, still available (see page 133).

after each change has been made. Be careful not to use force on the pedal, and to ensure smooth changes do not lift the foot from the pedal until the clutch has been re-engaged.

With regard to the carburettor controls, the throttle is opened by *inward* twisting of the grip and the air lever is also pulled inwards to open. To retard the ignition, pull the lever inwards. To ensure a quick start from cold, close the air lever completely, open the throttle a fraction of a turn (about $\frac{1}{16}$ in.), and move the ignition lever to about half retard. Then flood the carburettor, raise the exhaust valve lifter, kick the engine over, and drop the lifter smartly.

Tuning the Carburettor. All "Foxes" have a Bowden carburettor (type A) and full instructions for tuning will be found on page 44. The manufacturers have carefully adjusted each Bowden instrument after testing and it is seldom necessary to interfere with this setting. On 1934-5 "Foxes" the standard jets fitted are a 120 main and 75 pilot. Later "Fox" models have the same size main jet but a 55 pilot.

The standard jet sizes should give a petrol consumption of about 85 m.p.g., but if very economical running is desired, experiments should be made with the smaller size jets provided with the machine. Always remember, however, that too weak a mixture is liable to cause overheating. Except for changing the main jet and in rare instances the pilot jet, further tuning is limited to the setting of the throttle stop screw and the slow running adjuster screw. Faulty adjustment of the latter frequently causes heavy petrol consumption and it should therefore be very carefully set with a warm engine and the mixture control on the handlebars (the air lever) fully open. Screwing out the adjuster weakens the mixture and screwing it in enriches the mixture. Do not forget occasionally to remove the gauze filter situated by the feed and clean it and the filter cap thoroughly. Also verify that both the pipe lines are clear.

Sparking Plugs. For touring purposes the makers advise the fitting of an 18 mm. Lodge H1 or K.L.G. M60, or where 14 mm. plugs are specified, a Lodge H14 or K.L.G. F70. Keep the plug thoroughly clean and the gap at the electrodes adjusted to 0·018-0·020 in. on magneto models and 0·020-0·022 in. on coil ignition models (see notes on page 47).

Care of Contact-breaker, etc. On the 1934 "Red Fox" which has Miller coil ignition the contact-breaker is mounted on the timing cover but on all other models it constitutes part of the Lucas magneto. Lucas contact-breakers of recent design are of the face cam type as shown in Fig. 28 and comprehensive advice on its maintenance and the care of earlier rotating type Lucas and stationary type Miller contact-breakers is given on pages 48-52.

Cleanliness and correct adjustment of the gap at the contacts are most important. In the case of the 1934 "Red Fox," allow a gap of 0·020 in. and on the other "Foxes" a gap of 0·012 in. A feeler gauge of the right thickness is provided in the tool-kit. Where a magneto is fitted, do not forget occasionally to remove the h.t. pick-up and clean both this and the slip-ring below (see page 52). If the magneto chain requires retensioning, loosen the magneto base bolts and slide the magneto backwards on its platform until there is no more than $\frac{3}{16}$ in. slack in the chain.

Ignition Timing. The correct ignition timing (see page 53) for all 1934 and later "Red Foxes" and "Flying Foxes" with 490 c.c. J.A.P. engines is to set the contact-breaker points so that they commence to "break" with the piston 40 degrees or 17 mm. before top dead centre and the ignition lever fully *advanced*.

Miller Dynamo Maintenance. The subject of lubrication has already been discussed and the only other attention needed is in regard to the commutator which, like the contact-breaker, must be kept scrupulously clean. Here is an important warning: before touching the commutator first *disconnect the positive lead from the battery*, otherwise there is a risk of a short circuit causing the ammeter to be burnt out or the dynamo polarity to be reversed.

With a new dynamo no attention to the commutator is needed for several thousand miles, but afterwards it is advisable to remove the commutator cover about every 1000 miles and inspect the carbon brushes which must be absolutely clean and able to move freely in their holders. There must also be perfect contact between the brushes and the copper segments. To clean the brushes with a petrol moistened cloth, pull back each brush-retaining spring and remove the brush by pulling on its lead, being careful to see that the brush pressure spring is clear of the brush holder. Examine the brushes for wear and unevenness and true up if necessary. Generally it is best to replace the brushes before serious wear develops, as this prevents sparking which causes blackening of the commutator and an unsteady charging current. To clean a blackened commutator, press (with a piece of wood) fine glass-paper against the segments while rotating the armature. Should there be no blackening but just the accumulation of some grease and carbon dust, hold a cloth moistened in petrol against the segments and turn over the armature slowly (Fig. 40). If the segments are highly polished and of a *dark bronze* colour, leave them alone. Do not interfere with the cut-out except for very occasional cleaning of the contacts.

How to Retension the Belt Drive. To ensure smooth and vibrationless running at all speeds, an endless Dunlop belt of V-section drives the Miller dynamo off the crankshaft by means of pulleys (see Fig. 37). A simple method of adjusting the belt tension is provided. The armature is mounted eccentrically in its housing, and to retension the belt it is only necessary to loosen the dynamo strap-securing bolt and rotate the dynamo bodily anti-clockwise to tighten and clockwise to slacken. Keep the belt tensioned so that there is just no slack, but do not tighten beyond this point. Should oil accidentally get on the belt and cause slip, the remedy

FIG. 37. THE DYNAMO BELT SHOULD BE KEPT JUST TAUT
If the belt is excessively tightened, a strain is imposed on the armature

is not to tighten the belt but to clean it with a rag and petrol. If slip occurs due to wear of the rubber, renew the belt at once.

Care of Battery. An Exide 13 ampere-hour battery is provided on the A.J.W. machines under the saddle and is easily and instantly removable. To ensure a brilliant beam from the 8 in. or 7 in. Miller headlamp while riding by night it is imperative to pay regular attention to the battery, and this is particularly essential in the case of 1934 "Red Foxes" where current is drawn not only for the lights and horn but also for the coil ignition system. There are five essential points in battery maintenance. Here they are—

(1) Always keep the level of the electrolyte just above the tops of the plates.

(2) Top-up whenever necessary with pure *distilled* water.

(3) Never leave the battery in a fully discharged state.

(4) Make intelligent use of the headlamp charging switch.

(5) Occasionally check the specific gravity of the electrolyte with a hydrometer.

To Remove Battery. In order to top up the battery or check the specific gravity of the acid it is necessary to release the fixing strap and remove the battery from its mounting. On machines with low level exhaust pipes the complete battery can be readily detached, but on machines with high level pipes (i.e. on the 1935-7 "Flying Foxes") the exhaust pipe on the off-side prevents this being done and it is necessary to remove the battery lid before the battery can be lifted clear.

Topping-up. Examine the acid level at least every four weeks, and even more frequently in hot weather and tropical climates. Be careful not to hold a naked light near the vent holes. If the level is below the tops of the plates, add distilled water as required. This should be added just before a charge run, as the agitation due to running and the gassing will thoroughly mix the solution. If the solution has been spilled by accident, add diluted sulphuric acid of specific gravity equal to that remaining in the cells. When the inspection is carried out, hydrometer readings (specific gravity values) should be taken of the solution in one of the cells, and occasionally of that in all the cells. These readings are the most reliable method of indicating accurately the condition of the cells. Keep the battery connexions clean and free from acid. Smear well with petroleum jelly to prevent corrosion.

Charging Hints. The amount of charging needed is variable owing to various running conditions. If the light is poor and falls off when the machine is standing, charging should be immediately carried out. It is difficult to lay down rigid instructions on the question of charging, since it largely depends upon the extent to which the lamps are used. With the coil ignition models more charging is necessary than with the magneto ignition models, since the current is used for ignition and lighting. The following suggestion may serve as a rough guide: leave the switch in the "charge" position during the day for about 50 per cent of the night riding (a slight charge should flow to the battery when running with lamps on). Charging a battery after discharge raises the specific gravity, and discharging lowers the specific gravity. Place on charge, either by running the engine or using an independent electrical supply, immediately any battery whose specific gravity has fallen below 1·210. Take hydrometer readings whenever trouble is experienced with any part of the electrical system. *The correct specific gravity reading is* 1·285 to 1·300 in the case of the Miller batteries (fully charged at 60° F.).

How to Adjust Focus (Miller Headlamps). To detach the lamp front, release the spring clip at the bottom and pull the front off. To focus the bulb, insert it in the bulb-holder until the bayonet fixing pins are right home and give a further twist to the right. This will enable the bulb and holder to be slid backwards or

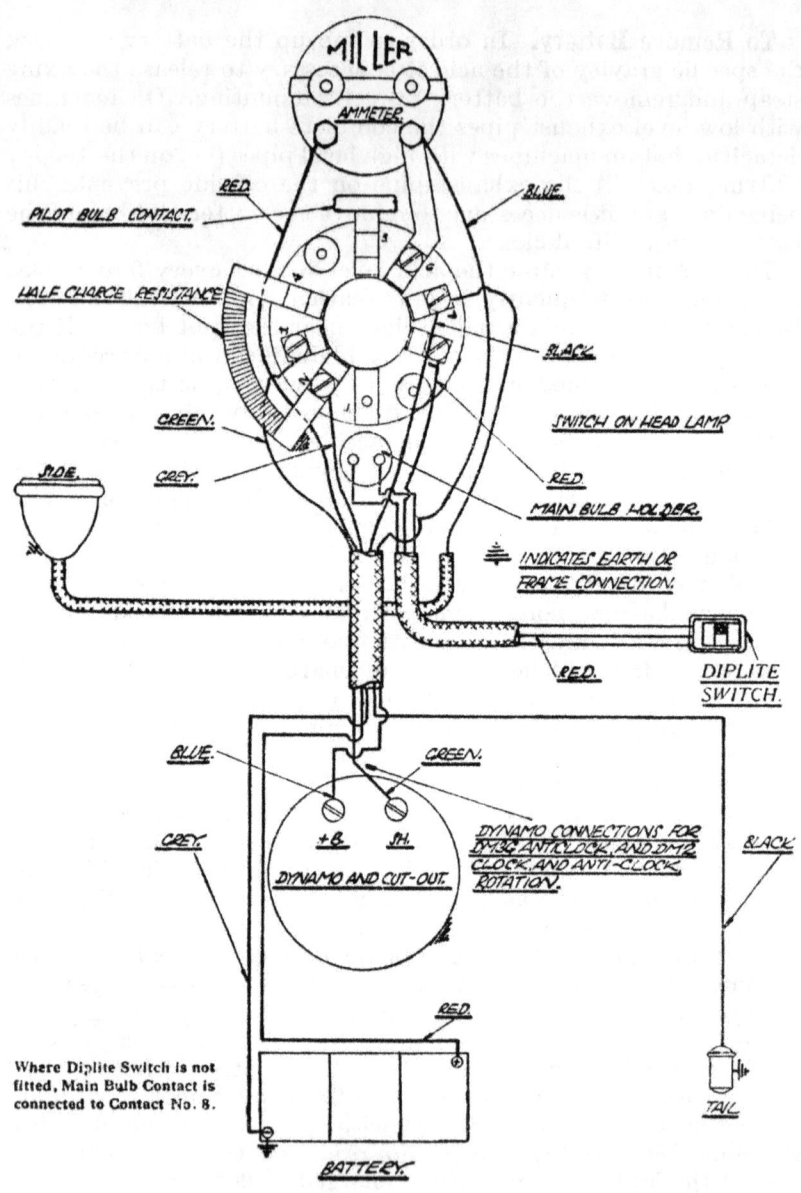

Fig. 38. Wiring Diagram for 1934 and Later A.J.W. "Foxes" with Miller Dynamo Lighting

HINTS FOR 1934-9 A.J.W. OWNERS

forwards until the correct focus is obtained. On releasing the extra twist, the bulb is securely held. A good method of focusing the headlamp is to take the machine to a level plot of ground and place it so that the lamp is 30 to 40 feet from a fence or wall and measure the distance from the centre of the headlamp to the ground and chalk on the fence or wall a mark at the same height. Then switch on the main bulb and note if the centre of the beam coincides with the mark. If it does not do so, loosen the headlamp bracket nuts and tilt the lamp as required. Then proceed to focus for intensity of light as described in the preceding paragraph.

Miller Bulb Replacements. The correct bulbs to fit are as follows. On magneto ignition models fit a 6V. 24/24W. double-filament main bulb and 6V. 3W. s.c.c. pilot, sidecar, and tail bulb. On coil ignition models fit a 6V. 18/18 W. double-filament main bulb and the above-mentioned pilot and tail bulbs. For the ignition tell-tale a 2·5V. flashlamp bulb is suitable.

Hints on Decarbonizing. Decarbonizing the 490 c.c. J.A.P. engine on a "Red Fox" or "Flying Fox" is perfectly straightforward and is fully dealt with in Chapter II. To make the job easy, the petrol tank should be taken right off by removing the front fixing bolt and the two bolts at the rear after disconnecting the petrol pipes and shutting the two taps. If on dismantling the cylinder head there are any signs of "blowing," renew or re-anneal the copper washer (page 31) and, after grinding-in the valves if necessary (page 25), set both valve clearances to 0·002 in. as described on page 34. Should any valve springs need replacement, the author advises the fitting of "Aero" springs. All J.A.P. engine spares can be had from Wimborne (see page 133) or from the engine manufacturers.

Cleaning Silencer. On 1934-7 "Flying Fox" models which have what appear to be straight-through exhaust pipes there is a Burgess sound-absorbing element in each pipe consisting of a long perforated tube packed with glass wool. This is apt to become choked, and, when decarbonizing, the mufflers which are fixed by a nut and bolt at each end should be removed and the carbon cleaned from the perforated holes with a stiff wire brush.

Gearbox Replenishment. An Albion heavyweight gearbox is fitted to most "Foxes" but some have a "Python" box. To prevent gearbox trouble, the level of lubricant should be inspected about every 1000-1500 miles, and if necessary replenished with engine oil (see page 1), preferably with Castrol "XL." In the case of the "Python" gearbox, replenish up to the level of the filling plug and in the case of the Albion gearbox the addition of a quarter of a pint every 1000 miles should be sufficient. On this gearbox the clutch sprocket, when free, runs on a ball race and occasionally a few spots of oil should be dropped down the side of the sprocket between the corks with the clutch disengaged. Also put a little oil on the lever end of the clutch rod. It is considered good practice to drain the gearbox after completing the running-in period and replenish with fresh oil.

Gear Control Adjustment. No adjustment is necessary on models with foot control, but on those models having hand control (i.e. the three-speed models) it is usually necessary to readjust the gear control after retensioning the primary chain. To adjust the control, remove the gear-rod yoke pin at the hand lever end and adjust the yoke end with the gear lever centrally placed in the second gear quadrant notch.

Adjustment of Clutch. Always allow a little backlash at the clutch handlebar lever (or $\frac{1}{32}$ in. between the ball in the clutch lever and the push-rod), but avoid excessive backlash which makes proper clutch disengagement difficult. Stretch in the Bowden cable can be taken up by means of the cable adjuster and also by means of the screw on the push-rod lever arm. On 1934-5 models the clutch spring pressure cannot be adjusted, but on later models the pressure can be adjusted by means of the four spring adjusting screws in the outer clutch plate. When new clutch corks become necessary, it is best to get them inserted by the makers as the faces need to be ground true. Six rubber segments in the clutch back-plate form the shock-absorber, and after a very big mileage it is desirable to renew the rubbers. If oil gets on the cork insert plates, clean them with petrol. See that the clutch sprocket is always kept in perfect alignment with the engine sprocket and that the primary chain is not too tight.

Care of Primary Chain. The primary chain on all models is completely enclosed. On 1934-5 "Foxes" it is lubricated by a pipe from the engine breather, but on later models it is positively lubricated, an oil feed being taken from the oil tank on "Red Foxes" and from the oil-way in the timing case cover on "Flying Foxes." A regulator is provided and this should be turned *three* notches (just before No. 1) which gives a supply of about six drops per minute. The primary chain usually needs retensioning during the first 1000 miles and afterwards much less frequently. Correctly tensioned, there should be $\frac{3}{8}$ in. to $\frac{1}{2}$ in. deflection with the chain in its tautest position. To adjust the chain tension, first remove the chain-case cover by disconnecting the rear brake rod, removing the foot-rest and unscrewing the two cover fixing bolts. Then on 1934-5 models loosen the gearbox fixing nuts and draw the gearbox backwards by means of the drawbolt until the correct chain tension is obtained. On 1936 and later models the gearbox can be pivoted the necessary amount by means of two adjusters screwed into each side of the slot in the gearbox casing. After adjusting the chain, check the gear control adjustment on a "Red Fox."

Care of Secondary Chain. The rear chain should always be kept clean, well lubricated, and properly tensioned. On 1936 and subsequent "Foxes" automatic lubrication from the engine breather is provided, but on 1934-5 models there is no means of lubrication. Whenever the chain shows signs of running dry some grease such as Price's "Rangraphine" or "Castrolease Graphited" should be rubbed into the chain with a stiff brush. Engine oil can be used but grease is much better as it is not thrown off by centrifugal force. About every 2000 miles the chain should be removed, cleaned in a bath of paraffin, hung up to dry, and then immersed in a bath of hot grease or tallow heated (until liquid) over a tin of boiling water. Do not remove the chain till the grease has cooled off.

With regard to chain tension, there should be $\frac{1}{2}$ in. to $\frac{3}{4}$ in. deflection with the chain in the tightest position, and to retension the chain it is only necessary to slacken the wheel spindle nuts and adjust the draw-bolts (which go over the wheel spindle) until the wheel is moved in the forward slotted fork ends the requisite amount. When adjusting the draw-bolts be sure that this is done uniformly on both sides, otherwise the wheel and sprocket alignment will be upset. To check the alinement, use a straight edge or a taut piece of string. If a chain has stretched very badly, remove a link. See that the spring link is fitted with the open end facing *away* from the direction of chain travel.

To Remove Rear Wheel. As the rear fork ends are slotted forward the rear wheel can be removed without disconnecting the chain. To remove the wheel, put the machine on the stand and lift up the hinged tail piece of the mudguard after loosening the two stay bolts. Next disconnect the rear brake rod and remove the brake-plate anchorage bolt. Then loosen the wheel spindle nuts enough to permit the chain draw-bolts to lift clear and drop the wheel forward. Finally, after lifting the chain off its sprocket, the wheel can be slid back and out.

To Remove Front Wheel. Put the machine on its stand and let down the front stand (situated under the crankcase on "Flying Foxes"). Then disconnect the brake rod, loosen the wheel spindle nuts, free the recessed washers, and allow the wheel to drop out of the fork ends.

Hub Lubrication and Adjustment. A good quality medium-bodied grease (such as "Castrolease Medium") should be injected through the hub nipples about every 3000-4000 miles. Avoid excessive lubrication, or grease may get on to the brake linings.

Should play develop in the cup and cone bearings, this can be taken up by means of the adjustable cone and lock-nut. On 1936 and later "Foxes" the adjustable rear wheel cone is inside the brake drum and the wheel must be removed in order to adjust the bearings.

Correct Tyre Pressures. To get the maximum life from the tyres and the best road holding, check the tyre pressures frequently with a pressure gauge and pump up to the correct pressure if necessary. Dunlop or Firestone tyres, 26 in. × 3·25 in., are fitted and the pressures for solo riding should be 16 lb. and 20 lb. per sq. in. for the front and rear tyres respectively. If a

FIG. 39. TESTING FOR PLAY IN THE STEERING HEAD

26 in. × 3·00 in. front tyre is fitted, add an extra 3 lb. per sq. in. For sidecar driving the correct pressures are 20 lb. and 26 lb. per sq. in. for front and rear tyres. For prolonged pillion work the pressure of the rear tyre should be increased by 2-3 lb. per sq. in.

Do Not Permit Play in the Steering Head. Check for play in the steering head after the first 500 miles and then at intervals of 2000-3000 miles. Adjustment is greatly simplified by the front stand fitted under the crankcase which takes the weight off the bearing and enables the steering freedom and play to be tested as shown in Fig. 39. No appreciable play or stiffness should be present and adjustment is made by loosening the bolt on the steering head clip and tightening or slackening the adjuster nut.

About every 1000 miles apply the grease-gun to the nipples provided for lubrication of the steering head bearings.

Looking After Front Forks. About every 500 miles inject some grease into the fork spindle lubricators until it begins to ooze out on both sides. Side play in the fork shackles may easily be felt by striding the machine and locking the forks over from one side to another. Adjustment is made by means of the adjuster nuts on the near-side after first loosening the locking nuts.

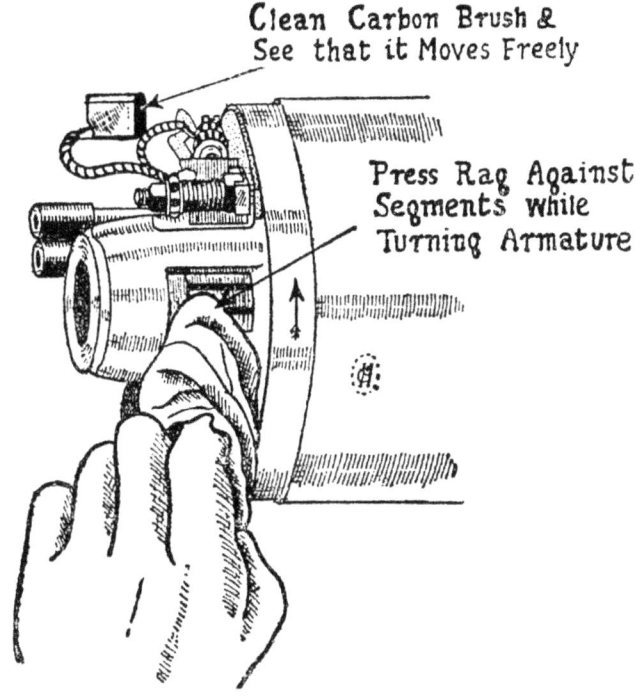

FIG. 40. SKETCH SHOWING COMMUTATOR END OF MILLER DYNAMO. THE SEGMENTS ARE BEING CLEANED WITH A RAG AND ONE OF THE BRUSHES IS SHOWN REMOVED

Do Not Neglect the Speedometer. There is a grease nipple on the speedometer gearbox on 1936 and later "Foxes" and the grease-gun should be applied about every 2000 miles.

Brake Cam Spindles, Control Levers, etc. Occasionally apply the oil-can to items such as the brake cam spindles, controls, etc. Oilers with spring cover clips are provided for the former.

Finally do not forget to check from time to time the tightness of the various frame and engine mounting bolts.

CHAPTER VI

CARE OF THE A.J.W. "GREY FOX"

THIS chapter deals with the handling, maintenance, and overhaul of the 1948-50 A.J.W. "Grey Fox," powered with the 494 c.c. S.V. vertical twin J.A.P. engine. The specification of this attractive mount is described on page 132.

The author is indebted to Mr. J. O. Ball, formerly a director of A.J.W. Motor Cycles, Ltd., for supplying some technical information, and the contents of this chapter should prove of considerable assistance to all "Grey Fox" owners. See also page 133.

Getting on the Road. The law does not permit you to venture forth on the public highway astride a "Grey Fox" (or any other motor-cycle) until you have attended to the preliminaries outlined below. You must—

(1) Insure against all *third-party* risks and obtain the all important "certificate of insurance." With a valuable machine like the "Grey Fox" it is obviously advisable to take out full comprehensive insurance.

(2) Obtain the registration licence and registration book (Form R.F. 1/2),* or renew the licence (Form R.F. 1/A).

(3) Obtain a "provisional" or driving licence (Form D.L.1).

(4) Have a speedometer fitted which will show when you are exceeding 30 m.p.h., within plus or minus 10 per cent accuracy.

(5) If you carry a pillion passenger, see that he or she sits *astride* a proper pillion seat securely fixed to the machine.

(6) Where you are *not* eligible for an actual driving licence, attach "L" plates to the front and rear of the machine.

All the above-mentioned forms are obtainable from a money order post office, but note that you cannot obtain an actual driving licence until you have reached the age of sixteen years and have complied with one of the following conditions—

(1) Have passed an official driving test (Form D.L. 26).

(2) Have held a driving licence prior to 1st April, 1934.

(3) Have obtained exemption from the prescribed driving test under the provisions of the Road Traffic (Driving Licences) Act, 1947.

---

* On the A.J.W. "Grey Fox" the engine number is stamped on the near-side of the crankcase, just above the light alloy cap covering the end of the camshaft. The frame number is stamped on the front of the steering head, and also on the near-side engine bearer cross member of the frame.

CARE OF THE A.J.W. "GREY FOX"

Is Riding Position Comfortable? On taking delivery of your "Grey Fox" it is always well worth while making sure that the riding position is the best obtainable having regard to your own particular physique and dimensions. The handlebars, and footrests, can both be adjusted within limits, and combined adjustments should be experimented with until the riding position is just right.

(*By courtesy of "Motor Cycling"*)

FIG. 41. VIEW OF A.J.W. "GREY FOX" WITH 494 c.c. S.V. VERTICAL TWIN J.A.P. ENGINE

To Adjust Handlebars. To adjust the position of the handlebars, slacken the four clamp securing set-screws and rotate the handlebars in the clamps until the most comfortable position of the grips is obtained. Afterwards be sure to retighten the clamp securing nuts firmly. It may be necessary to make a subsequent adjustment of the handlebar control levers. To do this, release the clips and swivel the controls relatively to the grips.

To Adjust Footrests. On the "Grey Fox" a dual adjustment is provided for. Each footrest can be adjusted for both reach and height after loosening the associated lock-nuts. The method of effecting the two adjustments is clearly indicated in Fig. 42. After making the required adjustment(s), see that the lock-nuts are firmly retightened.

The foot gear-change lever and the kick-starter crank are both fitted to splined shafts and it is possible to adjust their angle in relation to the footrests, if this is desired. The position of the rear brake pedal can also be adjusted to give the most comfortable position in relation to the nearside footrest (see page 97).

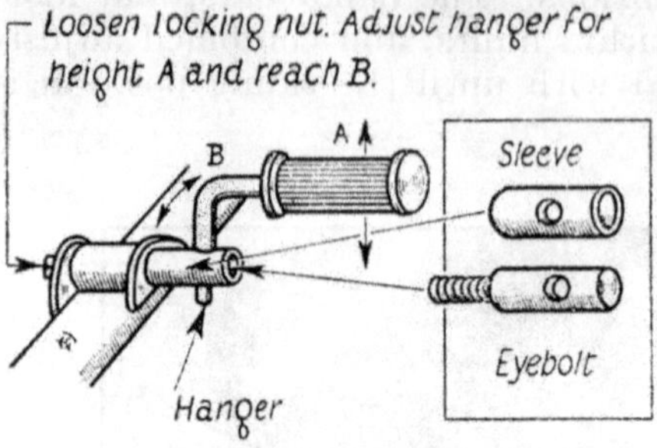

Loosen locking nut. Adjust hanger for height A and reach B.

Fig. 42. Each Footrest has Two Adjustments
Note the method of adjusting for reach and height

Starting Up the J.A.P. Engine. Observe the starting instructions given on page 69. For normal starting *from cold* open the throttle about one-eighth and close the air lever. If the engine is warm, open the air lever slightly. On all "Grey Foxes" the air lever is mounted beneath the saddle, a somewhat unusual position. On earlier 1948 models it opened downwards, but on all later machines the air lever opens *inwards*. See that the ignition lever in the centre of the lighting switch is switched on.

If the J.A.P. engine does not fire after two or three kicks (probably due to over flooding), open the throttle wide. It is very important not to over flood the Amal carburettor. Slight oozing of petrol from the float chamber is quite sufficient. Do not flood the carburettor with the "Grey Fox" on its stand, as there is a risk in this case of petrol running down the induction port.

Running-in the Engine. The S.V. vertical twin J.A.P. engine requires to be run-in for a somewhat longer period than is the case with a single-cylinder J.A.P. engine, and the advice given on page 69 should be carefully noted.

The makers of the A.J.W. "Grey Fox" do not advise that their machines be ridden at more than 40 m.p.h. during the first 500 miles. They also stress the importance of preventing the engine from labouring, changing down early, and frequently varying the loads on the engine and gearbox by altering the throttle openings often.

As the bearing surfaces become smooth and hard, the throttle openings can be progressively increased. A.J.W. Motor Cycles, Ltd., have suggested that during the first 200-300 miles you carefully attend to the following —

(1) Check the contact-breaker gap (see page 68) and, if necessary, make an adjustment. The fibre heel on the rocker arm beds down somewhat and may alter the gap.

(2) Inspect the primary and secondary chains for correct tension and adjust if required (see page 100).

CARE OF THE A.J.W. "GREY FOX"

(3) Check over the clutch adjustment. During the running-in period the plates invariably bed down to an appreciable extent.

(4) Verify the steering head adjustment, and adjust if slackness in the bearings exists (see page 101).

(5) Inspect the cable-operated controls for slackness. Some initial stretch of the Bowden cables usually takes place.

(6) Check over the front and rear brake adjustment (see page 97). Some bedding down of the brake linings is to be expected.

After the running-in period is passed, it may be found desirable to adjust the carburettor slightly, later on to decarbonize, and possibly to adjust the tappets, but these matters should only be attended to where really called for. Excessive "tinkering" with an engine which runs well is to be strongly deprecated.

Economical Cruising Speed. The makers of the A.J.W. "Grey Fox" consider that the most economical cruising speed is around 40-45 m.p.h. Some performance figures are given on page 131.

ENGINE MAINTENANCE

Correct Lubrication. Detailed instructions for the correct lubrication of the 494 c.c. S.V. vertical twin J.A.P. engine are given on pages 67-8. Check the oil level in the sump regularly. To avoid a faulty dip-stick reading, when using the stick, be sure that the "Grey Fox" is on *level* ground and that the filler cap (to which the dip-stick is attached) is *resting* on top of the filler neck. It must *not* be screwed home.

Drain and clean the oil sump about every 3000 miles as described on page 68. Do not forget to lubricate the contact-breaker cam occasionally. The dyno-distributor unit is also referred to on page 68.

Keep the Engine Clean. The importance of correct lubrication and keeping the engine thoroughly clean internally and externally cannot be over emphasized. Dirt is apt to mask defects and can accidentally enter the engine when it is being stripped down. It also accelerates rusting. Rusted cylinder block fins, besides being an eyesore, are detrimental to efficient heat dispersion by radiation. They should be kept clean and black.

To clean the cylinder block and cylinder head fins, use a stiff brush dipped in paraffin. Clean all aluminium alloy and bright surfaces with rags and paraffin, assisted by brushes where necessary. Use stiff brushes and paraffin to scour off all filth from the lower part of the crankcase.

Check Over Nuts Occasionally. It is a good plan to check over the various nuts for tightness at regular intervals, especially during the running-in period when some initial bedding down occurs. Pay special attention to the cylinder head and cylinder block securing nuts, also the engine plate nuts and the union nuts for the pipe connexions.

Suitable Sparking Plugs. It is best to run on a Lodge CB14, a Champion L-10S, or a K.L.G. F50. Weatherproof terminals and watertight plugs are referred to on page 142. Keep the plug clean and the gap adjusted to 0·020 in.-0·022 in. (see pages 47 and 52).

The Contact-breaker. Follow the instructions given on page 68.

Carburettor Tuning and Maintenance. Tuning and maintenance instructions for the Amal two-lever needle-jet carburettor are given on pages 38-44. On the A.J.W. "Grey Fox" engine the standard main jet size is 140, and the needle position should be so that the clip is in the *middle* groove. A 4/6 throttle valve is standard.

Cleaning Burgess Air Filter. On the "Grey Fox" engine a Burgess air filter replaces the Amal type referred to on page 69. No attempt should be made to run the machine with the filter removed, unless the above-mentioned carburettor setting is altered, otherwise the mixture will be too weak.

About every 2000 miles (at shorter periods in a dusty climate) the Burgess air filter should be removed and cleaned. Soak the gauze in petrol and vigorously shake until all dirt has been removed. Then dip the gauze in light oil, allow to drain, and replace.

Tappet Adjustment. Tappet adjustment (0·004 in., inlet; 0·006 in., exhaust) is referred to in detail on pages 69-70, and a shim adjustment is seldom called for.

Decarbonizing the Engine. Decarbonizing and grinding-in the valves are dealt with on pages 70-3. Removal of the cylinder head and cylinder block can be undertaken *without* removing the engine and gearbox unit from the frame, but some "Grey Fox" owners may prefer to remove the complete unit (see page 104) prior to taking off the cylinder block.

Removal of the petrol tank (see page 104) is quite unnecessary in order to remove the cylinder head, but its removal is a convenience when removing the cylinder block or engine and gearbox unit.

To Clean Burgess Silencers. Each of the two tubular Burgess silencers can be pulled out of its exhaust pipe after first undoing the four securing screws. To clean a Burgess silencer, and remove all soot and carbon deposits, force a stiff bottle brush through it.

Ignition and Valve Timing. For comprehensive instructions on timing the ignition and valves, see pages 74-6.

LUBRICATION OF "GREY FOX"

It is almost as important to lubricate the cycle parts of your "Grey Fox" properly as it is to lubricate the J.A.P. engine correctly. If you neglect the machine itself, you will not appreciate to the full the joy of a well cared for motor.

CARE OF THE A.J.W. "GREY FOX" 93

The Four-speed Burman Gearbox. All Burman gearboxes are initially replenished with grease by the makers. It is advisable every 1000-1500 miles to top-up the gearbox with 2-3 oz of soft grease. The grease should be inserted through the filler orifice which is accessible on removing the slotted domed cap, located (on the off-side) on the gearbox end cover. Rotation of the kick-starter will facilitate replenishment.

On *no* account use thick grease. Suitable greases for lubricating the Burman gearbox (and various cycle parts by means of the grease nipples provided) are as follows —
(1) Shell "Retinax" C.D.
(2) Mobilgrease No. 2.
(3) Price's Energrease C3.
(4) Castrolease "Medium."
(5) Esso Grease.

It is desirable to drain and flush out the gearbox about every 5000 miles and change the lubricant.

The Four-speed Albion Gearbox. In the case of the four-speed Albion gearbox fitted to many later "Grey Foxes," grease should *not* be used, as this may gain access to the oil-ways and thus obstruct the free passage of lubricant.

Every 500 miles or so top-up the Albion gearbox through the filler orifice with about a quarter of a pint of one of the following oils —
(1) Mobiloil BB.
(2) Castrol XXL.
(3) Shell X-100 SAE 50.
(4) Energol SAE 40 (Energol Auto 200, overseas).
(5) Regent Motor Oil 50 (Caltex Motor Oil 50, overseas).
(6) Essolube Racer (Essolube 50, overseas).

The clutch sprocket runs on ball bearings. You should lubricate these bearings occasionally by fully withdrawing the clutch and allowing a few spots of oil to drip down the side of the clutch sprocket between the corks. Also oil the clutch cable. Occasionally apply the grease gun to the nipple on the end of the shaft on which the gear change pedal operates.

Replenish Oil-bath Chain Case Regularly. The $\frac{1}{2}$ in. pitch primary chain runs totally enclosed in an oil-bath chain case. With the machine on level ground, remove the oil level plug regularly, inspect the oil level, and where necessary top-up the oil-bath with a light oil such as Single Shell, or Mobiloil Arctic, until the oil level reaches the lower edge of the inspection plug hole. The level plug is combined with the filler plug, except on some earlier export models. To remove the inspection plug, rotate the screwed knob so as to slacken the retaining spring, and then withdraw the plug.

Secondary Chain Lubrication. The $\frac{5}{8}$ in. pitch secondary chain is lubricated by splash from the oil-bath chain case provided for the primary chain. But since the secondary chain is protected only by a guard, it is advisable about every 2000 miles in summer and about every 1000 miles in winter to remove the chain from the gearbox and rear wheel sprockets and treat it in the following manner—

(1) Clean the chain thoroughly with paraffin.

(2) Hang the chain up and allow it to dry.

(3) Submerge the chain for approximately *five minutes* in a suitable receptacle containing molten tallow. If molten tallow is not available, soak the chain in engine oil for an hour or two.

(4) Permit excessive molten tallow to drain off the chain.

(5) Replace the chain on the sprockets.

Grease Wheel Bearings Annually. Once a year remove both wheels, dismantle the hubs, and re-pack the non-adjustable journal bearings with some soft grease (see page 93). First, however, remove *all* traces of the original grease.

Also the Steering Head Bearings. Re-pack the steering head bearings with soft grease (page 93) annually.

Lubrication of Dowty "Oleomatic" Front Forks. At weekly intervals give a few strokes of the grease gun with the latter applied to the nipples on the shrouds of the telescopic forks. For instructions, see page 116.

Unless oil is lost through gland failure, it is most unlikely that any topping-up of the Dowty front forks will be required, except perhaps about once every six months. Detailed instructions on topping-up procedure will be found on page 116.

The A.J.W. Rear Springing. At weekly intervals lubricate the rear fork ends with some heavy gear oil. Two grease nipples (see Fig. 51) are provided for the application of an oil gun.

Brake Lubrication. Occasionally (say, every 1000 miles) apply the grease gun to the nipple provided on the boss of the rear brake pedal arm. Also grease lightly the brake cam operating spindles to which the brake arms are attached. At the same time oil the exposed connexions of both brakes, and the cable ends, not forgetting the short length of cable used for the rear brake. Be very careful not to permit any oil or grease to get on to the brake linings.

Some brake cam operating spindles have a grease nipple provided, but others have only an oil hole. It is important to use only a *very little* grease on the cam spindles, otherwise some may get on the shoes and impair brake efficiency.

Speedometer Lubrication. The Smiths 120 m.p.h. trip-type speedometer fitted over the front forks requires no attention other than occasional lubrication of the speedometer flexible drive and the speedometer gearbox.

About every 3000 miles it is advisable to apply the grease gun to the nipple on the worm-drive speedometer gearbox which is situated on the off-side of the rear wheel. Use one of the greases mentioned on page 93.

Miscellaneous Oiling. Do not forget occasionally (say, every 1000 miles) to use the oil can on various parts which if allowed to become dry get stiff or are liable to corrode. For instance, oil

FIG. 43. TRANSMISSION SIDE VIEW OF 494 c.c. A.J.W. "GREY FOX"
A timing side view of the S.V. vertical twin is shown on page 131

the control lever pivots (do not forget the air lever beneath the saddle), and the ends of the control cables and nipples. Remember, too, to oil the pivots of the low-lift centre spring-up stand.

Oiling, except in the vicinity of vulnerable parts such as the contacts of the contact-breaker, the commutator, tyres, etc., can do no harm, and may, on the other hand, do a world of good. Oil, moreover, is cheap and easily obtainable.

CLEANING AND ADJUSTMENTS

Cleaning the J.A.P. S.V. vertical twin engine and its maintenance have already been dealt with. In the remaining pages of this chapter the "Grey Fox" motor-cycle components will alone be considered.

Cleaning the Machine. As in the case of the engine, thorough cleaning of your "Grey Fox" motor-cycle well repays the labour expended. It facilitates inspection and the making of routine adjustments. Moreover, if the enamelled parts and the plated surfaces are badly neglected, your machine will quickly assume a second-hand look, and serious rusting may occur.

On no account leave your mount over-night in a muddy and

soaking wet condition. If you cannot spare the time for thorough cleaning in wet weather, grease the machine all over before use. To remove filth from the lower part of the engine and gearbox unit, use a stiff brush and paraffin.

To Clean Enamelled Parts. Never attempt to rub or brush off caked mud when dry. Soak it off by means of a hose, being careful not to wet vulnerable parts such as the carburettor, battery, and

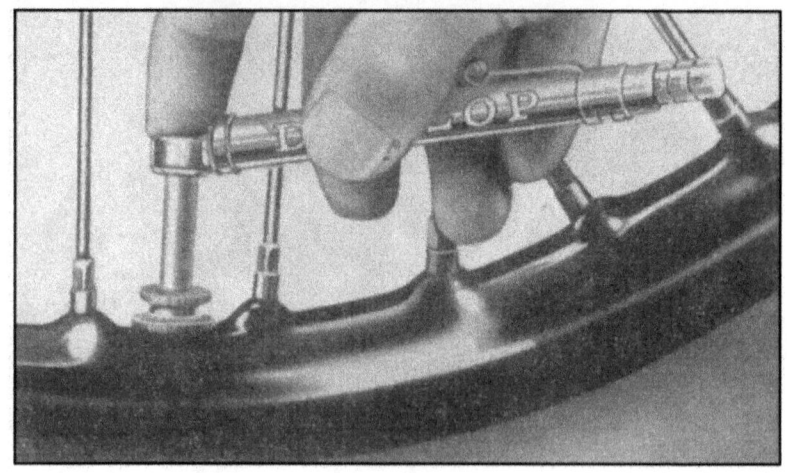

(*By courtesy of Dunlop Rubber Co., Ltd.*)
Fig. 44. Always Check the Tyre Pressures Like This

dyno-distributor unit. If a hose is not available, use a sponge, rags, and a pail of water.

After removing all dirt and mud, dry the enamelled parts with a chamois leather, and afterwards polish the surfaces with some soft dusters. To bring up the original lustre, use a good wax polish.

To Clean Chromium Plating. Light alloy parts can be brightened up with some metal polish, but this must *not* be used to clean chromium plating. To remove tarnish (salt deposits), clean the surfaces regularly with a damp chamois leather and then polish them with a soft duster. Some special compounds are available from accessory firms (see page 139) for cleaning chromium, and these can safely be used. Tarnish-resisting compounds are also available for winter use.

To Clean Rubber Gaiters. To clean the rubber gaiters which are fitted over the A.J.W. rear springs, use a soft rag dipped in petrol. This treatment will quickly restore their shine and colour.

To Clean Footrests and Tyres. A little black shoe polish brushed on to the footrest rubbers and the walls of your tyres will help to preserve them and prevent them becoming shabby looking.

CARE OF THE A.J.W. "GREY FOX"

Always Run on Correct Tyre Pressures. To obtain maximum comfort on your "Fox" and to extract the maximum mileage from your tyres, it is essential to check the tyre pressures regularly and pump up to the correct pressures where necessary. The correct pressure is 16 lb per sq in. for the front and rear tyres. If you are extra heavy, or wish to carry a pillion passenger, it is advisable to add an extra pound or two to the pressure.

Do not kick the tyres to estimate their pressure, but check the pressures weekly with a pressure gauge such as the Dunlop pencil type No. 6, Schrader No. 7750, or the Holdtite.

See that both wheels are kept truly aligned and examine the treads of the tyres occasionally for flints and small stones. These

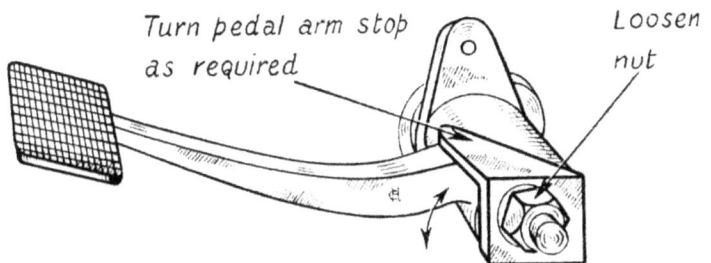

FIG. 45. ADJUSTABLE STOP FOR ALTERING REAR BRAKE PEDAL POSITION

should be prised out. Avoid excessive acceleration, prolonged large throttle openings, excessive braking, and "blinding" over bad roads. If you are unlucky enough to get a puncture and are not experienced in making repairs, the advice given in the Appendix may be of some assistance.

Brake Adjustment. Both brakes should be adjusted so that the wheels can be spun freely without any trace of binding, and so that the brake shoe linings contact the drums with small movement of the lever or pedal. Easily operated finger adjustment is provided for both brakes.

To take up slack in the front brake (cable) operation, screw out the knurled adjuster located in the top of the brake anchor arm. To eliminate slack in the rear brake (rod and cable) operation, remove the split pin and the clevis pin which holds the shackle to the rear brake pedal, and then turn the knurled adjuster as required. After making the adjustment, do not forget to replace the split pin which secures the clevis pin to the eye of the pedal.

Is Pedal Position Good? The position of the rear brake pedal relative to the near-side footrest can be adjusted to suit individual requirements. As may be seen in Fig. 45, the boss of the brake pedal arm abuts an adjustable stop on the brake pedal shaft.

To adjust the position of the stop, slacken the nut on the end of the shaft and turn the stop until the best brake pedal position is obtained. Be sure to re-tighten the stop securing nut afterwards.

No Internal Adjustment. No internal brake shoe adjustment is provided, and should the lining of a shoe become badly worn it must be renewed. Ferodo linings, already drilled for riveting, together with a complete set of rivets, are obtainable from the address given on page 133.

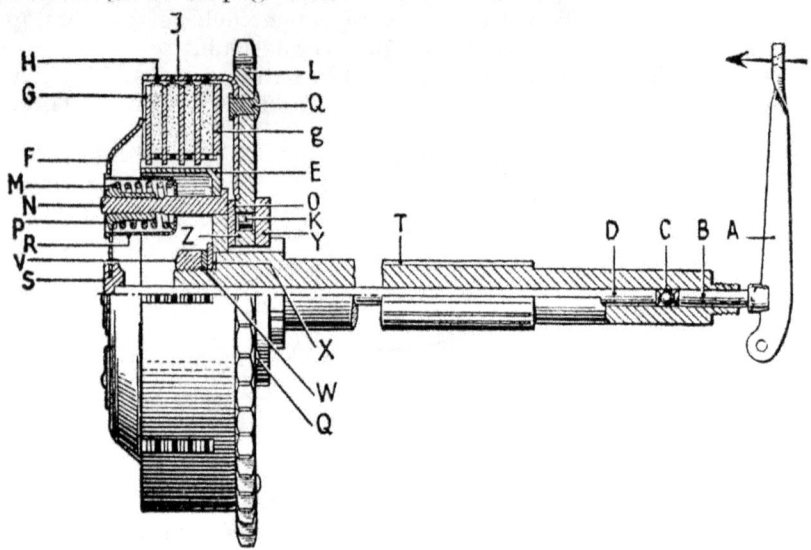

FIG. 46. DETAILS OF BURMAN MULTI-PLATE CLUTCH AND OPERATING MECHANISM (SEE ALSO FIG. 47)

```
A = Clutch operating lever          N = Stud for spring adjustment nut
B = Short steel plunger             O = Washer (thin) retaining roller bearing
C = Steel ball                      P = Spring adjustment sleeve-nut
D = Long thrust rod                 Q = Rivet
E = Clutch centre                   R = Spring cup (one of four)
F = Spring pressure plate           S = Pressure plate boss
G, g = Steel plain plates           T = Gearbox mainshaft (see Fig. 66)
H = Friction insert plates          V = Nut retaining clutch centre
J = Clutch case                     W = Spring washer
K = Roller bearing rollers (24)     X = Plain washer
L = Clutch sprocket                 Y = Washer (thick) retaining roller bearing
M = Clutch spring (one of four)     Z = Roller bearing ring
```

The Wheel Bearings. These are of the journal type and no adjustment whatever is provided or necessary. When the bearings become badly worn after thousands of miles, they must be renewed.

To Adjust Clutch (**Burman Gearbox**). Always maintain a little backlash (about $\tfrac{1}{16}$ in.) at the handlebar lever end of the Bowden cable. The cable gradually stretches and the friction inserts also become worn. Slackness should be taken up as soon as it develops. Two adjustments are provided for doing this.

CARE OF THE A.J.W. "GREY FOX"

To effect a normal adjustment, loosen the lock-nut and turn the small cable adjuster shown in Fig. 66 a few turns until the desired clearance at the cable end is obtained. After making an adjustment, be sure to re-tighten the lock-nut.

After a considerable mileage, wear of the friction inserts may be such that it is impossible to obtain a satisfactory clutch adjustment in the manner described above. In this case it is necessary to alter the angle of attack of the operating lever shown at C in

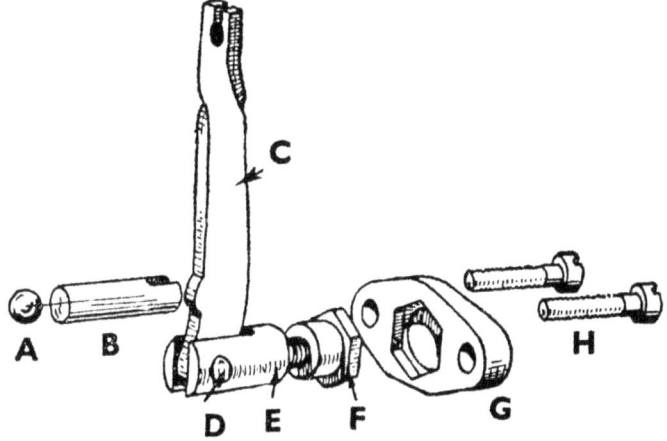

FIG. 47. CLUTCH-OPERATING LEVER ADJUSTMENT

The operating lever fork (E) slides in the kick-starter cover case, and its position is determined by the sleeve nut (F) locked by the cap (G) secured to the outside of the cover by the two screws (H)

A = Steel ball
B = Short steel plunger
C = Operating lever
D = Fulcrum pin
E = Fork for operating lever
F = Sleeve nut (adjuster)
G = Cap for sleeve nut
H = Cap securing screws

Fig. 47. To do this, remove the small cover G by unscrewing the two securing screws H and then to increase or decrease the clearance, turn the exposed sleeve nut F clockwise or anti-clockwise respectively. There should be $\frac{1}{32}$ in. clearance between the short steel plunger B and the nose of the operating lever C. One or two turns of the sleeve nut is generally sufficient to effect the required adjustment. Finally lock the sleeve nut F by replacing the cover G.

Clutch Spring Adjustment (Burman Gearbox). If the clutch adjustment is in order and in spite of this, clutch slip persists, the springs themselves may require an adjustment for tension. To do this, first remove the small screws situated round the rim of the oil-bath chain case cover and lift the cover off. This exposes the Burman clutch and the four sleeve-nut adjusters shown at P in Fig. 46.

To adjust the tension of the four clutch springs, first screw home half a complete turn each of the four adjuster sleeve nuts shown at P in Fig. 46. Then make a careful test to find out whether the clutch still slips. If it does, screw home each of the sleeve nuts a further half turn. Be very careful to adjust all four nuts *the same amount*. The normal adjustment is to screw home all the adjuster nuts fully and then unscrew them four complete turns. If it is necessary to screw nearly home the adjuster nuts, this shows that the springs have lost their tension, or else that the clutch inserts require to be renewed. Perhaps renewal of both springs and inserts is called for.

To Adjust Clutch (Albion Gearbox). As in the case of the Burman four-speed gearbox, wear of the clutch friction inserts (cork), and stretch in the operating cable, render an occasional adjustment necessary. Always maintain about $\frac{1}{32}$ in. clearance between the ball in the clutch actuating lever and the push-rod inside the gearbox mainshaft.

Check the clutch adjustment occasionally, and immediately if there is any indication of clutch slip (increase in r.p.m. and warming up of the plates). The actual adjustment comprises an adjuster pin and nut in the clutch lever at the kick-starter end.

Fitting New Cork Inserts (Albion Gearbox). It is highly desirable to have the faces of new cork inserts ground true, and this work is best entrusted to the Albion Engineering Co., Ltd., of Tower Works, Upper Highgate Street, Birmingham, 12.

Should you decide to fit new cork inserts yourself, first soak the corks in *boiling water* for a few minutes so as to make them pliable and easy to push into the holes. Insert the corks and tuck their edges in with a screwdriver. Then tap the corks flat and level.

To Re-tension Primary Chain. It is desirable to check the tension of the primary chain at regular intervals and to re-tension the chain if necessary. Re-tensioning is generally needed during the running-in period and subsequently at much longer intervals. Once the initial slight stretch has occurred, further stretching takes place very slowly as the chain runs under ideal conditions, being totally enclosed and partly submerged in oil.

To check the tension of the primary chain, first remove the inspection plug from the oil-bath chain case. Rotate the screwed knob so as to slacken off the retaining spring, and then withdraw the plug. Now turn the rear wheel over several times and check the tension of the chain in different positions. Correctly tensioned, it should be possible to deflect the chain with the fingers a *total* distance of $\frac{3}{8}$ in.-$\frac{1}{2}$ in., with the chain in its *lightest* position. If the chain is incorrectly tensioned, wear will be much accelerated.

To tighten the primary chain after checking its tension as just described, proceed as follows—

CARE OF THE A.J.W. "GREY FOX"

(1) Slacken off the off-side pivot bolt above the gearbox.
(2) Slacken off the near-side lower fixing bolt.
(3) Rotate the cam on the off-side lower fixing until the gearbox moves backwards the amount required to obtain correct chain tension (see opposite).
(4) Re-tighten the two gearbox fixing bolts.
(5) Replace the oil-bath chain case inspection plug.
(6) Re-tension the secondary chain as described below.

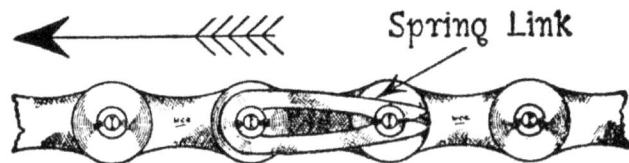

FIG. 48. THE SPRING LINK ON A CHAIN MUST ALWAYS BE FITTED LIKE THIS
The open end of the link must face opposite the direction of chain movement.

To Re-tension Secondary Chain. The chain is protected only by a guard and its tension is, therefore, readily checked. Re-tensioning is likely to be required a little more frequently than in the case of the primary chain, and the tension should be checked regularly, especially during the running-in period. Note that an adjustment is required after re-tensioning the primary chain, because primary chain adjustment involves moving the gearbox backward.

Chain tension is correct when the chain has a total up and down play of $\frac{1}{2}$ in.-$\frac{3}{4}$ in., with the chain in its *tightest* position. The A.J.W. "Grey Fox" has rear springing, and because of this it is essential to check and adjust the chain tension with the machine loaded, i.e. with *someone seated on the saddle*.

To tighten the secondary chain, first loosen the rear wheel spindle nuts, using the tommy-bar provided in the tool-kit. Then carefully tighten the chain by means of the draw-bolts provided on the rear fork ends. It is very important to move both draw-bolts *exactly the same amount*, otherwise wheel alignment will be upset.

Steering Head Adjustment. The instructions given on page 113 for adjusting the steering head bearings on Cottons fitted with Dowty "Oleomatic" front forks apply also to the "Grey Fox" which has similar forks fitted. Before checking or making the adjustment, make sure that the front wheel is raised quite clear of the ground. Note that the faintest suspicion of play in the bearings is preferable to adjusting the bearings too tightly.

Care of Lucas Dyno-distributor Unit. It is extremely unlikely that the unit on a new machine will require any attention for several thousands of miles, but the contacts should be inspected occasionally and their gap checked (0·018 in.–0·020 in.). Contact-breaker maintenance, including advice on lubrication, is dealt with on page 68.

To clean the commutator (see page 120) it is preferable to remove the dyno-distributor unit from the engine. Instructions for doing this are given on page 105.

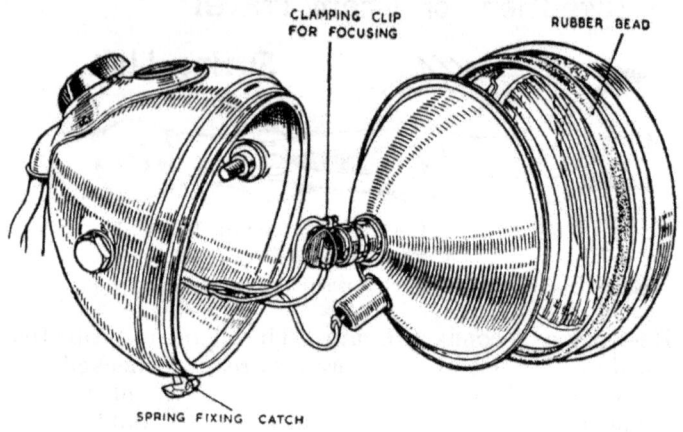

Fig. 49. The Lucas MU-42 Headlamp Used on the A.J.W. "Grey Fox"

The lamp front and reflector are shown removed. Focusing is effected by releasing the clamping clip and moving the bulb holder backwards or forwards as required

The Compensated Voltage Control Unit. The Lucas C.V.C. unit, which automatically controls battery charging, is mounted on rubber underneath the saddle on one of the frame cross members. It is of the same type as fitted to Cotton motor-cycles (see page 120), and should not be tampered with.

Care of Battery. The battery strapped to the "Grey Fox" is a Lucas lead-acid type PUW7E, and its maintenance is fully covered on pages 121–3. Check the level of the electrolyte regularly and top-up with distilled water as required. This does not necessitate the complete removal of the battery if one of the many forms of proprietary fillers is used. If you wish to remove the complete battery, proceed in accordance with the instructions given on page 105.

The Lucas MU-42 Headlamp. A view of the Lucas MU-42 headlamp fitted to the "Grey Fox" is shown in Fig. 49. The lamp has a double-filament main bulb and the usual pilot bulb for

CARE OF THE A.J.W. "GREY FOX" 103

parking purposes. Control of the double-filament bulb is by a dimming switch on the handlebars. The lighting switch, as may be seen, is mounted adjacent to the ammeter (see page 126) on top of the headlamp, and the ignition key is provided in the centre of the lighting switch. In all three switch positions the battery is on charge. The three positions are—

(1) "Off"—Headlamp (main, pilot bulbs), and rear lamp off.
(2) "L"—Headlamp (pilot bulb) and rear lamp on.
(3) "H"—Headlamp (main bulb) and rear lamp on.

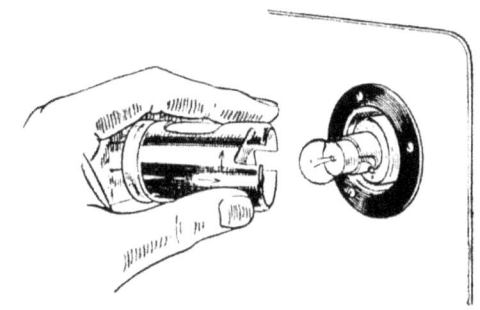

FIG. 50. REMOVING COVER FROM LUCAS MT211 REAR LAMP
The arrows indicate the direction of release movement

Focusing Headlamp. Note the advice on page 124 regarding the alignment and focusing of the DU-42 headlamp. These instructions apply also to the MU-42 headlamp except in regard to the removal and replacement of the lamp front and reflector.

To remove the front from an MU-42 headlamp, release the spring catch at the bottom of the headlamp and withdraw the front. The reflector is secured to the body of the lamp by means of a rubber bead and can be removed when the bead is detached.

When replacing the reflector, locate the thinner lip of the rubber bead between the rim of the reflector and the edge of the lamp body. When replacing the lamp front, locate the metal tongue in the slot at the top of the lamp, press the front on, and secure by means of the fixing catch.

The Lucas MT211 Rear Lamp. A Lucas MT211 rear lamp is fixed to the "Grey Fox" number plate. To remove the cover carrying the red glass, push in and turn in an *anti-clockwise* direction, as indicated in Fig. 50. When replacing the cover, engage the bayonet fixing, push in, and turn in a *clockwise* direction to secure the cover in position.

To Clean Lucas Lamps. Follow the advice given on page 129.

Bulb Renewal. Observe the instructions given on page 125, which are wholly applicable, except in regard to one particular;

disregard the reference to a No. 180 Lucas bulb. The correct types of Lucas bulbs to fit in the "Grey Fox" lamps are No. 70 and 200 for the headlamp main bulb and the rear lamp respectively. The pilot bulb should also be renewed by a No. 200.

Check Over the Wiring Harness Occasionally. Verify by an occasional close inspection that no chafing has occurred anywhere and that all connexions are clean and tight. Make quite sure that a good connexion exists at the forward rear mudguard fixing.

MISCELLANEOUS DISMANTLING

To Remove Petrol Tank. Removal of the A.J.W. petrol tank obviously facilitates removal of the cylinder block when decarbonizing the engine, but is not essential. Tank removal, however, is not necessary where the cylinder head only is removed. Removal of the tank is advised if you wish to remove the complete engine and gearbox unit from the frame.

To remove the petrol tank, first close both petrol taps and disconnect the pipe lines. Next withdraw the two set-screws at the front of the tank and the long bolt at the rear. Then carefully lift the tank off, raising it slightly backwards and upwards. Replacing the petrol tank should present no difficulty, but if the rear fixing bolt does not readily enter the rubber bush, moisten the bush in water so as to lubricate the rubber material.

Removing Engine and Gearbox Unit. This is advisable when undertaking a major overhaul, and some riders prefer to do it when removing the cylinder block (not essential). Before removing the engine and gearbox unit it is advisable to take off the petrol tank as described in the previous paragraph.

To remove the engine and gearbox unit from the frame, proceed in the following manner. Remove the battery (see page 105), the pipe lines, the exhaust pipes, the Amal carburettor, and the Burgess air filter. Also remove the outer half of the oil-bath chain case after removing the small securing screws located round its rim. Next remove the distributor cover and break the leads to the dynamo (fitted with connectors).

Although it is possible to remove the engine and gearbox unit with the front engine plates *in situ*, removal of the unit is facilitated by freeing the plates after loosening the securing nuts and sliding the plates outwards.

Remove the four nuts which secure the engine cradle to the frame and then push up the bolts until they are quite clear of the unit. Then lift the unit out of the frame *from the off-side*. When doing this raise the rear end slightly so as to prevent the lower rear sump bolts fouling the engine mounting, and then lift the unit out sideways. Lay the complete unit on a safe bench or on the floor pending strip, inspection, and overhaul. To re-assemble the engine and gearbox unit, proceed in the reverse order of dismantling.

To Remove Dyno-distributor Unit. First remove the cover from the engine timing case, also the dynamo driving chain, and the nut securing the dynamo driving sprocket. Then with the extractor provided in the tool-kit, loosen the dynamo driving sprocket itself. Slacken the nut which grips the band clip (see Fig. 36) round the body of the dynamo alongside the front engine mounting. Now disconnect the wiring leads attached to the dyno-distributor unit and remove the Lucas unit from the *near-side*.

When replacing the dyno-distributor unit, do not tighten the nut securing the band clip round the dynamo until *after* the dynamo driving chain is replaced and the timing adjusted (see page 74).

Removing Lucas Battery. Some riders prefer to remove the Lucas PUW7E battery when checking the acid level, topping-up, and taking specific gravity readings (dealt with on pages 122-3). To remove the battery, first undo the nuts on the vertical rod and so free the battery retaining strap. Slide the strap backwards, take off the battery lid, and remove the battery itself. A rubber pad is provided beneath the battery and it is *essential* to see that this pad is always replaced, otherwise the battery may suffer from the effects of excessive vibration.

To Remove Oil-bath Chain Case Cover. Remove the small screws situated round the rim of the cover and lift off the outer half of the oil-bath chain case, i.e. the cover. Allow all oil to drain off into a suitable receptacle, otherwise a horrible mess will inevitably occur.

Dismantling and Removing Burman Clutch. Referring to Fig. 46, remove all the four clutch spring adjustment sleeve-nuts (P). Next remove the four clutch springs (M) and the spring pressure plate (F). Now withdraw the four friction insert plates (H) and the five steel plain plates (G, g). Remove the nut (V) retaining the clutch centre (E) and also the spring washer (W) and plain washer (X). Disconnect the primary chain. Then withdraw the clutch centre, clutch case (J), and clutch sprocket (L) together.

To Remove Oil-bath Chain Case. Having removed the chain case cover, the primary chain, and the clutch, as previously described, remove the engine sprocket from its splined sleeve, using a suitable extractor. This gives access to four nuts on the studs holding the chain case to the engine main shaft boss (on the crankcase). Remove these four nuts and also the bolt holding the rear of the chain case to the engine and gearbox cradle. Then lift off the chain case.

Removing and Replacing Front Wheel. Instructions for removing and replacing the front wheel in the Dowty "Oleomatic" front forks are given on page 116. A point to note in the case of the "Grey Fox" is that replacement of the front wheel is facilitated by tilting the wheel slightly towards the *off-side* when inserting it in the front fork legs. This assists engagement of the brake anchor arm with the off-side leg.

To Remove and Replace Rear Wheel. First disconnect the rear half of the rear mudguard by removing the two short $\frac{5}{16}$ in.

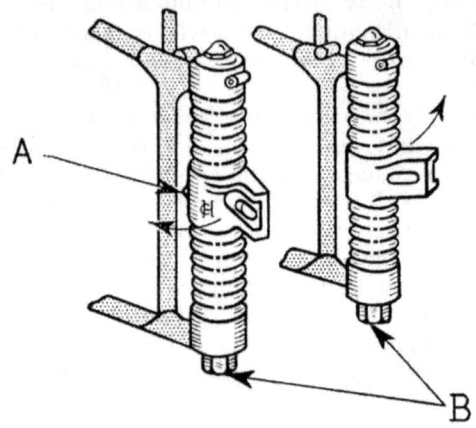

FIG. 51. PRIOR TO REMOVING OR REPLACING THE REAR WHEEL, OPEN OUT THE REAR FORK ENDS AS INDICATED

At weekly intervals heavy gear oil (see page 94) should be injected through the two nipples, one of which is shown at *A*. Do not tighten the two Oddie nuts shown at *B*

bolts connecting the front and rear halves. Also remove the two long $\frac{5}{16}$ in. bolts securing the bottom of the stays supporting the rear half. Then remove the rear half of the mudguard (complete with number plate) and lay it on the saddle.

Take out the clevis pin from the front shackle preferably, or from the rear shackle, of the rear brake cable. Next slip the cable out of the slotted frame abutment. Also disconnect the speedometer cable from the gearbox situated on the off-side of the rear wheel.

Remove the rear wheel spindle nuts and open out the rear fork ends (see Fig. 51) sufficiently to allow for the rear wheel being removed. Lift the secondary chain clear of the rear wheel sprocket and remove the rear wheel itself. The reassembly of the rear wheel and mudguard rear half should be effected in the reverse order of removal. When using a spanner on the rear wheel spindle nuts, make quite sure that the nuts are done up really tightly. This is most important.

CHAPTER VII

HINTS FOR COTTON OWNERS (1934 ON)

THE general specification of all four-stroke Cottons is very similar and engine capacities range from 122 c.c. to 600 c.c. The majority of Cottons* have J.A.P. engines but on the 122 c.c. model a Villiers engine is fitted. It is not proposed, however, to deal with the two-strokes. This chapter covers 1934-52 models.

Cotton Engine Lubrication. Machines of large capacity are in most cases provided with (non-adjustable) dry sump lubrication, but many of the smaller capacity models have (adjustable) wet sump lubrication. For full maintenance instructions see pages 5 and 9 respectively. On wet sump models drain and flush out the crankcase every 2500-3000 miles, and on dry sump models clean out the oil tank and gauze filter every 1000-1500 miles.

Miller " Magdynamo," Dynamo, Lucas " Maglita " Lubrication. Where Miller equipment is specified, see notes on page 12. In the case of the Lucas "Maglita," place a spot of oil on the steel cam and another drop in the holes under the contact-breaker and in the lubricator at the driving end every 1000 miles. See page 13.

The Cotton Controls. The position of the controls is the same as on the A.J.W. (see page 77) and the lighting switch is mounted on the headlamp. The carburettor controls operate by inward movement, but this does not apply to the ignition lever on all models (Lucas, inward; Miller, outward). To adjust the controls for starting from cold, follow the advice given on page 41 and below respectively for Amal or Bowden carburettors. See page 88 *re* getting on the road.

Tuning Amal Carburettor. If an Amal carburettor is fitted, tune it as described on page 41

Tuning Bowden Carburettor (Types A and B). Follow the tuning instructions given on page 46. Referring to Fig. 25, it should be emphasised that apart from altering the main jet size, and rarely that of the pilot jet, tuning of the Bowden carburettor should be confined to the setting of the throttle stop screw and the slow-running adjusting screw M. In no circumstances interfere with the full jet (A) or the total jet (F).

Starting from Cold (Bowden Type A). Follow the instructions given on page 46, in the first paragraph under the heading "Tuning for Slow-running (Type A)."

---

* Cotton motor-cycles are made by the Cotton Motor Co., of Gloucester.

Starting with Warm Engine (Bowden Type A). Move the mixture control lever (on the handlebars) to the normal or fully *open* position, open the throttle about $\tfrac{1}{16}$ in., and approximately half retard the ignition. Do *not* flood the carburettor. Then proceed to start up in the usual manner.

The Starting Device (Bowden Type B). With the Bowden type B carburettor there is only one handlebar-operated control (the

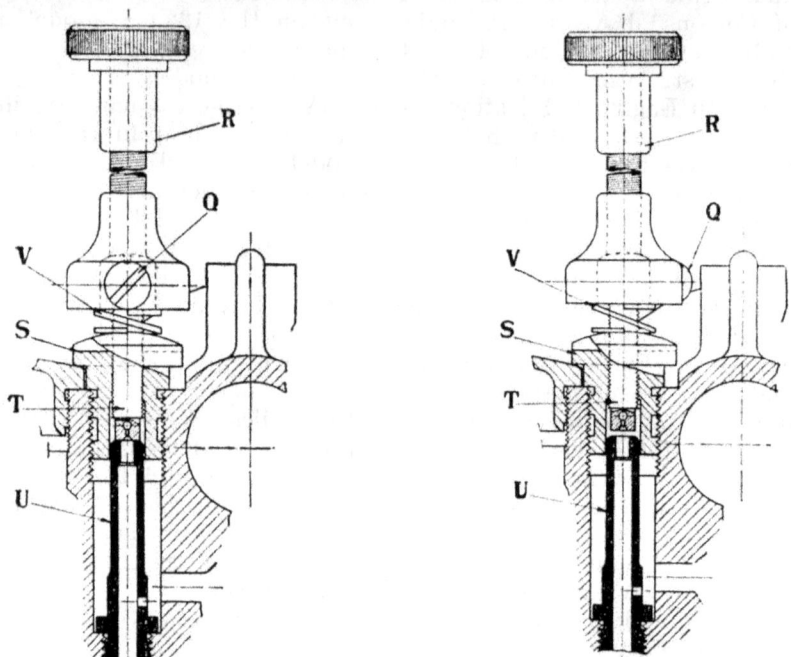

Fig. 52. Bowden Carburettor (Type B) Starting Device

In the left-hand illustration the control knob (R) has been turned to the "NORMAL" position for starting up a warm engine and for all normal running. In the right-hand illustration the control knob (R) has been turned to the "RICH" position for starting up a cold engine. The screw (T) contains the "pilot jet" orifice

throttle), the starting device (see Fig. 52) having a control knob (R) fitted to the carburettor itself. This knob is prevented from turning under vibration by means of the spring (V), and thus the "pilot jet" screw (T) is kept stationary in the jet cap (S) while the engine is running. A large pilot jet is fitted and the "pilot jet" screw (T) in effect takes over the normal duty of the pilot jet (U). As in the case of the pilot jet (G), used on the type A carburettor (see Fig. 25), the screw (T) is calibrated in c.c., and its head is stamped for size.

HINTS FOR COTTON OWNERS (1934 ON)

Referring to Fig. 52, when the "pilot jet" screw (T) seats on the jet (U), as shown in the left-hand illustration, the mixture is "NORMAL," the petrol being delivered to the engine via the calibrated hole in the jet screw (T). On the other hand, when the jet screw (T) is clear of the top of the jet (U), as shown in the right-hand illustration, the mixture is "RICH" for starting, as indicated by the arrow on top of the knob (R).

Starting from Cold (Bowden Type B). Open the throttle about $\frac{1}{16}$ in., retard the ignition about half-way, and turn the knob on the starting device to the "RICH" position, indicated by the arrow on the knob. Do *not* flood the carburettor unless the temperature is *very* cold. Now kick the engine over compression and start up. When the engine has become warm, turn the knob of the starting device to the "NORMAL" position.

Starting with Engine Warm (Bowden Type B). The procedure is the same as for starting from cold (see previous paragraph), except that the knob of the starting device must be turned to the "NORMAL" position before starting up. The carburettor must *not* be flooded.

Suitable Plugs. For advice on what plugs to use and how to keep a plug in good condition, see pages 47-8. Note that on Cotton coil ignition models a slightly larger gap at the electrodes is advisable than on magneto ignition models.

The Contact-breaker. On all Cotton models the contact-breaker is incorporated on the generator itself. Keep the gap at the contacts adjusted to 0·010 in., 0·019 in., 0·017 in., or 0·012 in. in the case of a Lucas "Maglita," Miller dynamo, Miller "Dynomag," or Lucas "Magdyno" respectively. Full information on contact-breaker maintenance will be found on pages 48-52.

Ignition Timings. The correct ignition timings for different J.A.P. engines are tabulated on page 55 and instructions for retiming the ignition will be found on pages 53-7.

Dynamo Maintenance. For hints on dynamo lubrication, see page 12. Where a Miller "Dyno-mag" or dynamo is provided, attend to the commutator and brushes as described on page 79. Where a Lucas "Maglita" is fitted, examine the brushes every 2000-3000 miles and see that they are clean, free from oil, and slide freely in their guides. Do not disturb the primary of the ignition coil. For "Magdyno" instructions, see pages 13, 50-2, and 119.

Lucas Coil Ignition. Certain 1934-52 Cotton models (e.g. 250 c.c. S.V.) have Lucas or Miller coil ignition fitted. The care of the Lucas dynamo and battery are dealt with on pages 119 and 121. Lubricate the dynamo as described on page 12.

The contact-breaker on Lucas coil ignition models is of the type shown in Fig. 53 and is attached to the dynamo. Keep the gap between the contacts at 0·010 in.–0·012 in. Where an adjustment is required, make this as described at the bottom of page 50.

Smear the surface of the cam lightly about every 3000 miles with some Mobilgrease No. 2 or, if not available, use clean engine oil. At the same period remove the contact-breaker lever and smear its pivot lightly with the same lubricant.

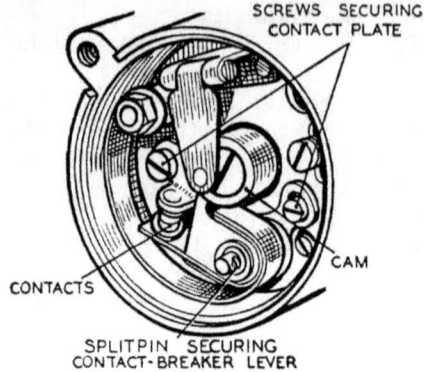

FIG. 53. LUCAS CONTACT-BREAKER (PRE-1950 COIL IGNITION)

The contact-breaker shown is of the stationary type and only the cam rotates. On 1950–2 250 c.c. S.V. Cottons the dynamo and contact-breaker are of Miller design

Do Not Forget the Coil. It is easy to forget this "static" item completely. See that the coil housing is kept clean, especially between the terminals, and make sure that the terminal connexions are kept done up tightly.

The Lucas Warning Lamp. On coil ignition models (Lucas and Miller) a red warning lamp is provided on the headlamp to inform you whether you have accidentally omitted to switch off the ignition when leaving the engine stationary. Failure to switch off (with the contacts of the contact-breaker closed) will run down the battery.

In the above circumstances the warning lamp shows a *red* light. It also lights up when the engine is ticking over. After much use the bulb is liable to burn out, but this does not in any way interfere with the ignition. But for obvious reasons it is desirable to renew the bulb as soon as possible. To remove the old bulb, detach the lamp front and reflector and unscrew the bulb. The correct bulb to use is a Lucas No. 970 (2·5 volt, 0·2 amp).

Retensioning Generator Chain. Always maintain about $\frac{3}{16}$ in. slack in the chain. On Cottons with a Lucas "Maglita" or Miller "Dyno-mag" retensioning of the chain entails moving the generator backwards on its slotted platform, but on coil ignition models the chain can be tightened by rotating the dynamo in its housing, the armature being eccentrically mounted. On the "High Camshaft" models automatic tensioning is provided for the generator chain, the Weller method being used.

The Battery. Where Miller equipment is specified, follow the maintenance instructions given on pages 80–1 (with the exception of the paragraph relating to battery removal). These instructions also apply to Lucas lead-acid batteries used in conjunction with the "Maglita" and "Magdyno," but it should be

HINTS FOR COTTON OWNERS (1934 ON)

noted that the correct specific gravity reading for Lucas batteries is 1·280–1·300 when fully charged at 60°F. See also page 121.

Bulb Replacements. The correct Miller replacements are given on page 83. In the case of Lucas "Maglita" equipment, fit a 6V. 12/12W. double-filament main bulb, a 6V. 3W. s.c.c. pilot, sidecar, and tail bulb. Focusing can be carried out for Miller lamps as described on page 81. See also page 125.

Decarbonizing. On some Cotton models, owing to the inclination of the engine in the frame and the space provided by the sloping tank tubes, it is not essential to remove the petrol tank in order to decarbonize. But it greatly facilitates decarbonizing to remove the tank by removing the four bolts which secure it. Instructions for dismantling and decarbonizing the side-valve, overhead-valve, and "high camshaft" J.A.P. engines will be found in Chapter II. Valve grinding is dealt with on pages 25–30. When valve spring replacements become necessary, the fitting of "Aero" or other first-class valve springs is advised. After decarbonizing and valve grinding, check the valve clearances as described on page 33. The tubular silencer cannot be dismantled for cleaning.

To Remove Engine from Frame (350 c.c., 500 c.c., 600 c.c., O.H.V.). If undertaking a complete overhaul it is desirable to remove the complete engine from the frame. To do this, first remove the exhaust pipe(s) and the Amal carburettor. Next remove the bolt securing the front engine plates to the front down tube of the frame. Also remove the three bolts securing the rear engine plates to the crankcase. Then lower the engine from the frame without disturbing the gearbox.

If the gearbox is to be taken off, or has already been removed, remove the bolt securing the front engine plates to the front down tube of the frame, and also three of the ½ in. frame cross-bolts. Then remove the engine, complete with the rear engine plates.

Maintenance of "High Camshafts" and Vertical Twin. The two "high camshafts" and also the S.V. vertical twin Cotton (not put into general production) all have a general specification (as regards the motor-cycle itself) similar to that of the other Cottons, and the appropriate instructions in this chapter apply. The S.V. vertical twin *engine* is dealt with fully in Chapter IV.

Gearbox Lubrication. Burman three- and four-speed gearboxes (with the shock-absorber incorporated in the clutch) are used on Cottons, and on new machines they are charged with sufficient grease for 1000 miles running. At the end of this period and subsequently at intervals of 1000–1200 miles 2–3 ounces of grease should be inserted through the filler orifice after removing the metal cap on top of the gearbox. Avoid excessive lubrication or grease may be forced out of the bearings; it is best to keep the box about *two-thirds* full. Suitable greases to use are Wakefield's "Castrolease Medium," Gargoyle "Mobilgrease No. 2," Shell Retinax CD, Esso Grease. To assist filling, turn the gears over with the kick-starter and in very cold weather add a little engine oil. Occasionally the various joints in the gear change mechanism should be lubricated, and the same applies to the clutch operating rod, the clutch lever, and the Bowden cable. See also page 136. Engine oil is advised for latest B52 gearboxes.

Adjustment of Gear Control. With foot control no adjustment is needed. With hand control, adjustment after retensioning the primary chain can be readily effected by screwing up or down the lower yoke end on the rod until the gears mesh with the gear lever placed centrally in second or first gear quadrant notch in the case of three- and four-speed gearboxes respectively. On most Burman gearboxes the provision of internal indexing facilitates adjustment, as this makes it possible to feel engagement.

Clutch Adjustment. There should be about $\frac{1}{32}$ in. clearance between the clutch push-rod and the ball in the operating lever. Adjustment can be made by means of the cable stop and lock-nut, and a further adjustment is provided by the screw adjuster in the centre of the clutch outer member. On later B52 gearboxes the lever has a fulcrum adjustment (Fig. 47). The clutch springs are adjustable but the screw heads should be kept approximately flush with the outer member. When adjusting, tighten each screw half a turn at a time as even tightening is essential. Keep the clutch control lubricated, and for notes regarding the cork inserts and sprocket alignment, see page 84.

Dismantling Burman Clutch. Unscrew the spring adjusters and remove the springs and spring cups. Then remove the spring plate and withdraw the other plates. To withdraw the clutch bodily, take off the spring plate and unscrew the nut which secures the clutch body to the castellated mainshaft.

Care of Transmission. The primary chain is well enclosed and automatically lubricated by the engine breather, but the secondary chain requires to be periodically greased and cleaned as described on page 94. Keep the chains tensioned so that there is $\frac{3}{8}$ in. to $\frac{1}{2}$ in. and $\frac{1}{2}$ in. to $\frac{3}{4}$ in. deflection in the front and rear chains respectively. Adjustment of the front chain is by moving the gearbox backwards or forwards by means of the usual draw-bolt, and adjustment of the rear chain is by accessible adjusters on the outside of the rear fork ends which, unlike the A.J.W., are rearward slotted. Note the remarks on page 85 regarding alignment.

To Remove Primary Chain-case. To remove the cover from the oil-bath chain case it is only necessary to remove *one* nut. To remove the chain case itself it is necessary on earlier models to

HINTS FOR COTTON OWNERS (1934 ON)

undo *two* securing nuts, the chain case being secured at the front to a crankcase boss and at the rear to the chain stay end.

On all later models removal of the chain case entails the removal of *one* nut at the rear and *four* nuts at the front.

Wheel Removal. The rear wheel is removed in the usual manner after disconnecting the chain and rear brake rod and loosening the spindle nuts. To facilitate removal the tail piece of the rear mudguard is detachable. The front wheel (girder forks) is fitted in slotted fork ends and the anchor plate is slotted to receive the anchor bolt. Removal of the wheel is self-obvious. See page 116.

Hubs and Tyres. Lubricate the ball-bearing hubs as described on page 85 and take up any play which may develop by means of the adjustable cones and lock-nuts. As regards tyre pressures, suitable solo pressures for most Cottons with Firestone or Goodyear tyres are 16 lb. and 20 lb. per sq. in. for front and rear (26 in. × 3·25 in.) tyres respectively. For prolonged pillion work add 3 lb. per sq. in. to the pressure of the rear tyre. For tyre repairs, see Appendix.

Is Saddle Position Good? Often a slight adjustment of the saddle position makes for more comfortable riding. On most Cottons there is a small adjustment for height possible, and also a considerable backward and forward adjustment. To make the required adjustment it is only necessary to loosen the saddle securing clip which is secured by one bolt and nut.

The Speedometer. About every 2000 miles apply the grease-gun to the grease nipple provided on the speedometer gearbox.

Cleaning a Cotton. Refer to the advice given for cleaning an A.J.W. "Grey Fox" (see page 96), but disregard the paragraph relating to rubber gaiters used for rear springs.

To Adjust Steering Head. It is considered desirable to check for play in the steering head bearings after the first 500 miles and then regularly at intervals of 2000-3000 miles.

On all Cottons when testing the steering head for play you should lift the front wheel clear of the ground by inserting some packing beneath the crankcase of the engine. This takes the weight off the steering head bearings and permits the steering freedom and play (if any) to be tested. There should be no perceptible stiffness or slackness present.

On Cotton motor-cycles provided with girder or pressed steel type front forks, to adjust the steering head bearings, first slacken the bolt securing the steering head clip and then tighten or loosen the adjuster nut as required to obtain the correct adjustment.

On Cottons with Dowty "Oleomatic" type front forks (fitted at no extra charge on all 1952 models) the steering head adjustment is very similar to the adjustment on the girder type forks. First loosen both clamp bolts on the fork crown fitting (see Fig. 55) and also the pad bolt on the handlebar clip lug. Then adjust the steering head nut as required. After making the adjustment, re-tighten firmly the pad bolt and the two clamp bolts.

Steering Head Lubrication. The steering head bearings are packed with grease by the makers and this should suffice for about 5000 miles when the bearings should be repacked. Grease nipples are provided on some early machines, and occasional application of the grease gun is desirable.

Front Fork Adjustment (Girder Type). On Cotton machines with pressed-steel front forks (e.g. 250 c.c. S.V.) there is no adjustment for play in the fork shackles. In the case of the tubular girder type front forks, however, any undue play can be taken up by means of the adjusting nuts between the fork links and fork tubes. The lubrication of the forks (other than those of the Dowty type) is as referred to on page 86 for the A.J.W. forks.

DOWTY "OLEOMATIC" FRONT FORKS

Dowty "Oleomatic" front forks are fitted on many 1949 and later Cottons as an alternative to girder type forks. They are also fitted as standard on the 1948-50 S.V. vertical twin A.J.W.

The "Oleomatic" front forks (details of which are shown in Figs. 54 and 55) combine air springing and oil damping. The air springing permits of considerable deflection to combat normal road irregularities, and at the same time enables all shocks to be absorbed without undue total movement of the forks occurring.

The motion of the synthetic rubber cushions in oil ensures practically constant and even damping of the forks in both directions and also absorbs any shock caused by full extension of the fork legs. Too rapid closing on compression is prevented by oil cushions between the internal top fittings and the pistons. Very little maintenance attention is needed in respect of the "Oleomatics."

Use Only Dowty Inflation Valve Cores. The Dowty inflation valve (shown at *B*, Figs. 54 and 55) is provided with a special core which opens at low pressure and is fitted with oil-resisting rubber seatings. In no circumstances fit a normal tyre insert, because the chemical action of oil rapidly causes natural rubber seatings to perish. You can obtain genuine Dowty valve core replacements from Dowty Equipment, Ltd., of Cheltenham, or from the motor-cycle firm concerned, or from accessory firms (see page 139).

To Inflate and Adjust to Load. On the front of each lower sliding tube there is a *red dot*. The two red dots should coincide with the bottom edges of the fork leg shrouds when the forks are correctly inflated with the rider seated on the saddle (with pillion passenger, if carried).

To obtain correct inflation, first slightly over inflate the forks by removing the dust cap from the inflation valve and applying an ordinary tyre pump to the valve. Pump in only a little air. Next sit on the saddle, with the feet on the motor-cycle footrests.

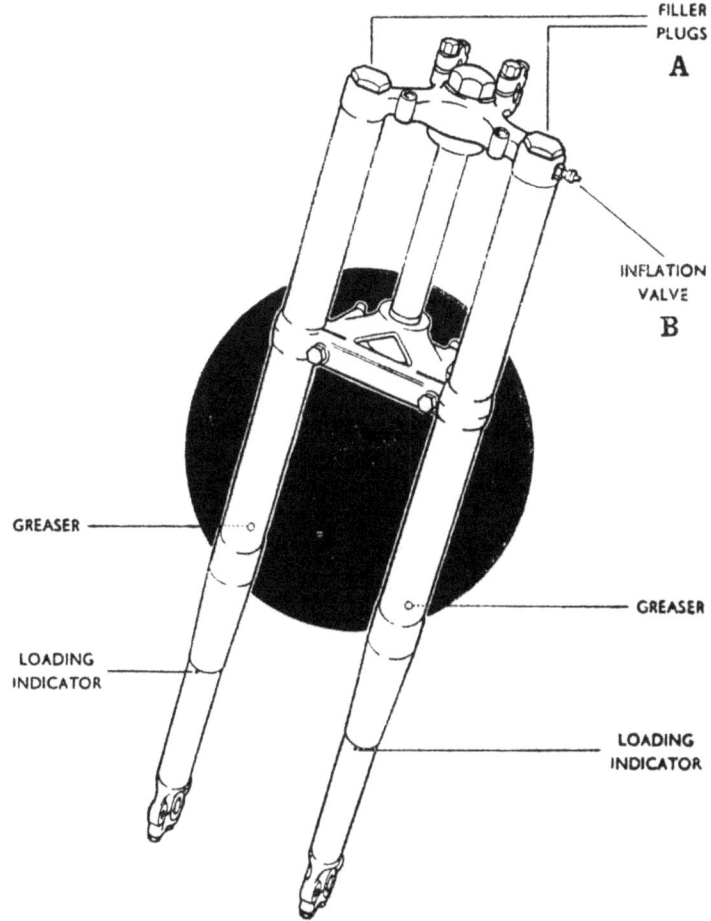

FIG. 54. VIEW OF DOWTY "OLEOMATIC" FRONT FORKS

These forks are fitted to many J.A.P. engined motor-cycles, and the sketch shows the essential points concerned with maintenance. Fig. 55 shows a partly sectioned and exploded view

Balance yourself and the machine in the most convenient manner.

Then release the air in small amounts by depressing the stem of the inflation valve until it is found that the red dots align with the bottom edges of the shrouds. Afterwards replace and tighten the valve dust cap.

How to Top-up "Oleomatics." Do not top-up unless "bottoming" occurs with the forks correctly inflated. During the operation it is important to pay attention to absolute cleanliness. First remove the dust cap from the inflation valve (*B*, Figs. 54, 55). Next permit *all* air to escape by depressing the valve stem. The fork legs will in consequence close up.

Now pack up the crankcase of the engine in such a manner that each fork leg is closed to the extent of *one inch from the fully closed position.* Remove both filler plugs (shown at *A* in Figs. 54, 55) and replenish each front fork leg with one of the following lubricants: Wakefield's Castrolite; Shell X-100 SAE 20/20W; Mobiloil Arctic; or Esso 20. Afterwards screw home the two filler plugs.

Remove the packing from under the crankcase and depress the inflation valve so as to enable surplus oil to drain away and the forks to close completely. Finally inflate and adjust to load (see previous paragraph), and replace the dust cap on the inflation valve.

First Filling. On new Cotton or A.J.W. machines the front forks are correctly filled and inflated. Except where the oil has become accidentally contaminated during topping-up, or refilling after dismantling the forks, it is quite unnecessary to change the oil throughout the life of the motor-cycle. If complete refilling with one of the above-mentioned lubricants is undertaken, considerably more oil must be inserted than is the case when only topping-up.

Greasing Instructions. Grease the bottom bearing in each fork leg weekly, and use only a high-grade grease. Greasing is very important to ensure a perfectly free fork action. Each greaser (see Fig. 54) is located at the rear of the outer tube, at the lower bearing. Surplus grease automatically escapes through vent holes in the sides of the outer tubes, below the fork crown.

Check Tightness of Nuts and Bolts Occasionally. This is important to the road worthiness of the front fork assembly, and on no account should the steering tube pad bolt be allowed to become slack. If it does, the alignment of the forks may suffer.

To Remove Front Wheel from "Oleomatics." First insert some suitable packing beneath the crankcase so as to extend the fork legs fully and raise the front wheel clear of the ground. Also disconnect the front brake cable at the brake drum. Next slacken the two nuts which locate the front wheel spindle cap on the brake drum side (see Fig. 55). Screw back the front wheel spindle nut about *two complete turns.* Then remove both front wheel spindle locating caps and allow the wheel to slide clear of the fork legs. To prevent damage, hold the wheel with one hand as it comes clear.

To Replace Front Wheel in "Oleomatics." Place the front wheel in position and screw up the four nuts securing the front wheel spindle locating caps, *finger tight only.* Next tighten the

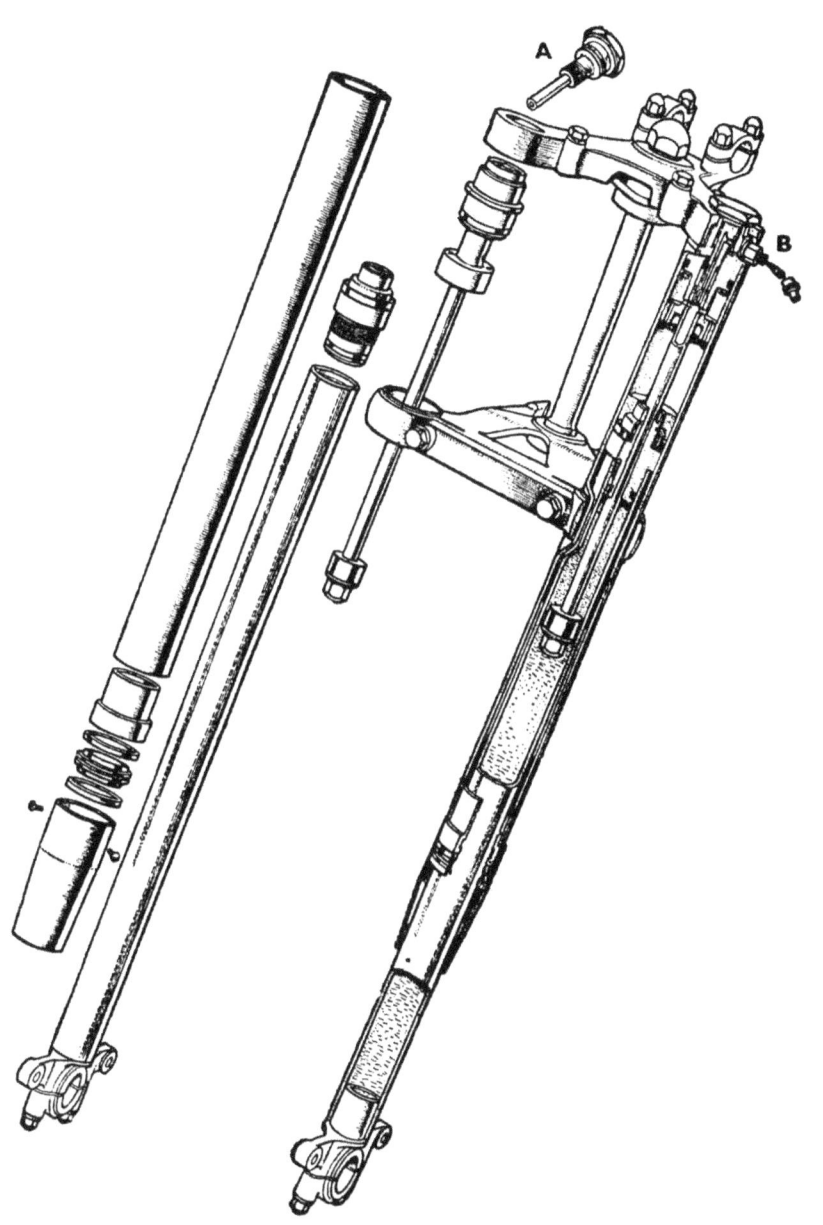

FIG. 55. "OLEOMATIC" FRONT FORKS (1949 ONWARDS)
(*By courtesy of "The Motor Cycle"*)

front wheel spindle nut on the *brake drum side*. This has the effect of holding the wheel firmly against the side of the spindle fitting. Now tighten the front wheel spindle cap securing nuts firmly on the brake drum side. During the above procedure it is assumed that the front wheel is raised clear of the ground by packing placed beneath the crankcase.

Remove the packing from beneath the crankcase and bounce the front forks several times on the ground. Then tighten the two nuts securing the near-side front wheel spindle locating cap. The purpose of the procedure just described is to ensure that the lower tubes of the front forks slide quite freely in the outer tubes. For this object a small clearance is provided between the front wheel spindle fitting and the shoulder on the spindle ferrule on the near-side.

LUCAS LIGHTING EQUIPMENT

Lucas electric lighting equipment has been and is fitted to numerous J.A.P. engined motor-cycles. On 1934-9 Cotton motor-cycles Miller lighting equipment was specified to a greater extent than Lucas equipment, and on 1934-9 A.J.W. "Foxes" Miller lighting sets were used exclusively. The production of Miller sets, however, temporarily ceased during hostilities, and practically all 1945-52 Cottons (except 1950-52 250 c.c. S.V.) have Lucas equipment fitted.

Outline of Equipment. On motor-cycles not provided with coil ignition, Lucas equipment includes a "Magdyno" with detachable dynamo, or else a separate dynamo where a magneto is fitted. In both cases the dynamo is of similar design and on 1937 and later models its output is controlled automatically by a compensated voltage control (C.V.C.) unit attached to some part of the frame (to the saddle pillar on Cottons).

Current from the dynamo is conducted to a Lucas lead-acid battery (generally type PUW7E) strapped to a platform beneath the saddle and thence fed as required to a large diameter Lucas headlamp (type DU-42 on most Cottons and A.J.W.s). A panel incorporating a lighting switch and centre-zero ammeter is fitted to the top of the headlamp which has a double-filament main bulb and a pilot bulb for parking purposes. The dimming switch for the double-filament main bulb is located on the left-hand side of the handlebars. The rear lamp fitted to most Cottons and some other machines is a Lucas MT110 or MT111.

Where Lucas coil ignition is provided (e.g. some pre-1950 250 c.c. S.V. Cottons) the dynamo and battery are similar to those used on magneto ignition models, but an ignition key is provided in the centre of the lighting switch, and a *red* warning lamp is included in or near the ammeter (see page 126) to indicate whether the ignition has been left on when the machine is stationary. With

HINTS FOR COTTON OWNERS (1934 ON)

coil ignition the battery, of course, supplies current for both lighting and ignition.

CARE OF THE DYNAMO

An Important Precaution. Precautions are unnecessary for inspecting the commutator, but on making adjustments to the wiring circuit, it is essential to take steps to prevent accidental "shorting." Disconnect the lead from the lighting switch to the Lucas battery *positive* terminal. Push back the rubber shield and then unscrew the cable connector. When doing this be sure that the cable does not make contact with any metal part of the frame, otherwise a "fat" spark will indicate that the battery *was* well charged! When reconnecting the lead, pull the rubber shield well over the connector.

Dynamo Overhaul. It is a good plan every 10,000 miles to entrust the dynamo or dynamo portion of a "Magdyno" to a Lucas service depot or agent for dismantling, cleaning, servicing, and lubrication. Lubrication is referred to on page 12.

Inspection of Commutator and Brushgear. The Lucas dynamo or dynamo portion of a "Magdyno" will run satisfactorily for thousands of miles with scarcely any attention other than occasional inspection of the commutator and brushgear. It is advisable once a season, or about every six months, to remove the metal band from the dynamo and make a careful inspection.

The Commutator Brushes. The brushes must make good electrical contact with the commutator. They must be absolutely clean and able to move freely in their box type holders, on holding back the retaining springs and gently pulling the leads and then releasing them. There must also be perfect contact between the brushes and the copper segments of the commutator; the brush faces in contact with the segments should be uniformly polished. Clean the brushes with a petrol-moistened cloth after removing them. To do this, pull back each brush-retaining spring (see Fig. 3) and remove the brush by pulling on its lead, being careful to see that the brush pressure spring is clear of the brush holder.

Examine the carbon brushes for wear and unevenness, and true them up if necessary. Generally it is best to replace the brushes *before* serious wear develops, as this prevents sparking, which causes blackening of the commutator and an unsteady charging current.

If Lucas brushes become so badly worn that it is necessary to remove them, this can easily be done as follows: Release the eyelet on the brush lead by unscrewing the hexagonal nut or screw at the terminal; then, holding back the spring lever out of the way, withdraw the brush from its holder. Renew with genuine Lucas brushes.

The brush springs should be inspected occasionally to see that they have sufficient tension to keep the brushes firmly pressed against the commutator when the dynamo is running. It is particularly necessary to keep this in mind when the brushes have been in use a long time and are very much worn down.

It is unwise to insert brushes of a grade other than that supplied with the dynamo, or to change the tension springs. The arrangement provided has been made only after many years' experience, and will be found to give the best results and the longest life. It is really best when the brushes become so worn that they no

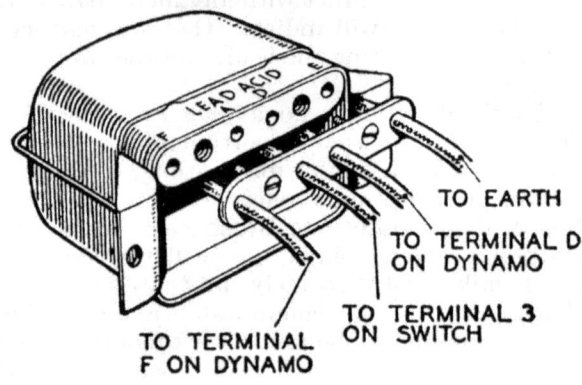

Fig. 56. Lucas Cut-out and Regulator Unit Connexions

longer make good contact, to have new brushes fitted at a Lucas service depot, as this ensures the brushes being properly "bedded."

Cleaning Commutator. The surface of the commutator segments should be kept clean and free from oil or brush dust, etc. Should any grease or oil work its way on to the commutator through overlubrication, it will cause not only sparking, but, in addition, carbon and copper dust will collect in the grooves between the commutator segments.

The best way to clean the commutator is, without disconnecting any leads, to remove from its box-holder one of the main brushes and, inserting a fine duster, hold it, by means of a suitably-shaped piece of wood, against the commutator surface, causing the armature to be rotated at the same time. If the commutator has been neglected for long periods, it may need cleaning with fine glasspaper, but this is more difficult to do, and should not be necessary if it has received regular attention. The segments should be *dark bronze* and highly polished.

Compensated Voltage Control (C.V.C.). Compensated voltage control is provided in conjunction with most 1947 and later Lucas dynamos and "Magdynos." The C.V.C. unit consists of a cut-out

HINTS FOR COTTON OWNERS (1934 ON)

and voltage regulator unit neatly housed in a box attached to the frame (the saddle pillar on 1937 and later Cottons). The unit is connected between the dynamo and battery and sees to it that the battery is automatically charged the right amount by varying the dynamo output according to the state of charge of the battery and the load imposed on it.

Current is prevented from flowing back from the battery to the dynamo at low r.p.m. by means of the cut-out which opens. As soon as the r.p.m. rise high enough to enable the dynamo to charge the battery, the cut-out closes and completes the circuit.

In all three lighting switch positions (see page 124) the Lucas dynamo gives a controlled output and thus relieves you of responsibility in regard to charging. The regulator begins to operate when the dynamo voltage reaches about 7·3 volt. During daylight running with the battery well charged and the switch in the "Off" position, the dynamo gives only a trickle charge, and the ammeter reading is unlikely to exceed 1–2 amp. There is no danger of overcharging.

The regulator provides for an increase of dynamo output as soon as the lamps are switched on. The effect of switching the lamps on after a long run with the battery voltage high is often to cause a temporary discharge reading at the ammeter, but fairly soon the voltage falls and the regulator responds, thereby causing the output of the dynamo to balance the load of the lamps.

When the battery is in a discharged state, the regulator increases the dynamo output and restores the battery to its normal state of charge in the shortest possible time.

Do Not Disturb C.V.C. Unit. The unit is sealed by the makers, as it does not need adjustment once it is correctly set. The only conceivable trouble is oxidizing or welding together of the contacts, owing to accidental crossing of the dynamo field and positive leads. Be careful if making wiring alterations (see page 119). Referring to Fig. 56, make sure that the C.V.C. unit connexions are correct, tight, and that the insulation is sound.

Should you fit a Lucas Nife battery in place of the lead-acid type, you must fit a new regulator to ensure a good charging rate with a discharged battery. You are advised to have the change-over made at a Lucas service depot or agent, and to visit a depot or agent whenever any serious electrical fault develops or if the dynamo under charges or over charges the battery.

CARE OF THE BATTERY (LEAD-ACID)

Neglect of the Lucas battery quickly brings trouble, and correct attention in regard to its maintenance is *vitally* important. Upon it depends the lamps and horn, and also the ignition on coil ignition models.

How to Top up the Cells. Examine the acid level about once a month, and even more frequently in tropical climates. Unscrew the battery clamping screw and remove the battery. Then take off the battery lid and remove the three vent plugs. Inspect the hole in each vent plug and make certain that it is not obstructed. A choked vent plug hole will result in an increase of pressure in the cell owing to "gassing," and this may cause trouble.

Wipe the top of the battery clean with a rag and also verify that the rubber washer fitted beneath each vent plug, to prevent leakage, is in position. After wiping the top of the battery, either destroy the rag or wash it thoroughly, using several changes of water. See that a supply of clean distilled water is to hand.

Be careful not to hold a naked light near the vents. If the level is below the tops of the separators, add *distilled* water* as required to bring the level correct. This should be done just before a charge run, as the agitation due to running and the gassing will thoroughly mix the solution. Acid must not be added to the electrolyte unless the solution has been spilled. If the solution has been spilled by accident, add diluted sulphuric acid of specific gravity equal to that in the cells.

Check Specific Gravity Monthly. About once a month, hydrometer readings (specific gravity values) should be taken of the solution in each of the cells. The method of doing this is shown in Fig. 57. The Lucas hydrometer contains a graduated float which indicates the specific gravity of the battery cell from which a sample of electrolyte is taken.

After a sample has been taken and checked, it must, of course, be returned to the cell. The taking of S.G. readings with a hydrometer is the most efficient way of ascertaining the state of charge of the battery. The S.G. readings should be approximately the *same for all three cells.* Should the reading for one cell differ substantially from the readings for the others, probably some acid has been spilled or has leaked from the cell concerned. There is also a possibility of a short-circuit between the battery plates. In the latter case it will be necessary to return the battery to a Lucas Service depot or agent for attention.

Under no circumstances must the battery be permitted to remain in a discharged condition for long, or serious deterioration will occur. After checking the S.G. readings and topping-up the cells, wipe the top of the battery and remove any spilled electrolyte or water; replace the three vent plugs and the battery lid. Then fit and tighten the battery clamping screw.

---

* The distilled water, unlike the acid, is lost gradually by evaporation. Bottles of distilled water can be obtained from most garages and from chemists, and topping-up effected with a Lucas battery filler.

If the battery is not going to be used for some time, leave it at a service station where it will receive periodic attention.

Concerning Battery Connexions. Always keep the battery connexions clean, free from corrosion, and tight, otherwise the ammeter readings will *not* indicate the true state of charge of the battery. To prevent corrosion they should be smeared with petroleum jelly.

Correct S.G. Readings. With Lucas batteries fitted to Cotton, A.J.W., and other machines, the specific gravity readings at an acid temperature of approximately 60°F. should be: 1·280–1·300, battery fully charged; about 1·210 battery half discharged; below 1·150, battery fully discharged.

Never leave the battery in a discharged state for any appreciable period. A low state of charge often is caused through parking the machine for long periods with the lighting switch in the "L" position, unaccompanied by much daylight running. The remedy is, of course, to undertake more daylight running and to keep the switch in the "Off" position as much as possible until the battery regains its normal state of charge. If overcharging occurs, have the setting of the compensated voltage control unit checked.

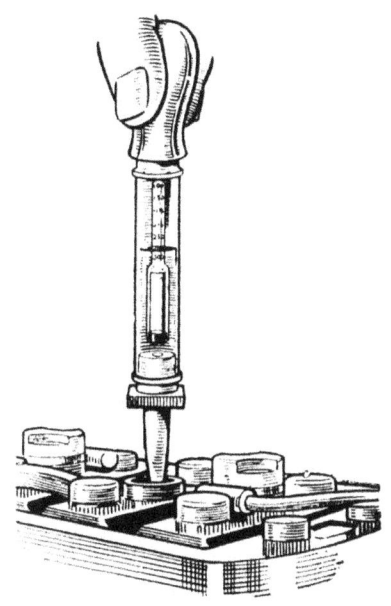

FIG. 57. USE OF LUCAS HYDROMETER TO CHECK SPECIFIC GRAVITY OF BATTERY ELECTROLYTE

Lucas Jelly-acid Battery. The foregoing instructions apply only to a Lucas lead-acid type battery. In the event of a jelly-acid type being used, add a *tablespoonful* of distilled water about once a month, and then allow the battery to stand for *two hours*. Afterwards draw off any surplus liquid on the top of the jelly.

CARE OF THE LAMPS

The headlamp instructions which follow apply to the Lucas DU-42 headlamp and all other Lucas "D" type lamps fitted to Cotton, A.J.W., and other machines with Lucas dynamo or "Magdyno" lighting, and compensated voltage control.

The Lucas DU-42 Headlamp Switch. As may be seen in Fig. 58, the lighting switch is mounted on a panel on top of the headlamp just behind the ammeter. The switch has three positions, and in all three the dynamo is charging so long as the engine is running.

The three switch positions are as follows—
"OFF"—All lamps switched off.
"L"—Headlamp (pilot bulb) and rear lamp, on.
"H"—Headlamp (main bulb) and rear lamp, on.

Is Headlamp Alignment Correct? Incorrect headlamp alignment and/or an out-of-focus main bulb give reduced road illumination and are liable to dazzle other road users. Both faults are simply rectified.

To check the headlamp alignment, take your motor-cycle to a straight, level stretch of road, turn the lighting switch to the "H" position, and operate the dipping switch so that the main driving light is switched on. The beam of light should, if alignment is correct, be straight ahead and parallel to the road or slightly below the horizontal. If the headlamp is mounted so that the beam of light is elevated or projects too much on the road, slacken the two side fixing-screws which secure the headlamp to its brackets and then tilt the headlamp slightly down or up until correct alignment is obtained. Afterwards tighten the two lamp fixing-screws firmly.

Correct Focusing is Important. On all new machines the double-filament main bulb is carefully focused to give the best illumination. Provided that genuine Lucas bulbs of the correct wattage and number are fitted as replacements (see page 126) subsequent re-focusing should not be necessary. Where a Lucas bulb is not available, or the focusing adjustment has been disturbed, it is necessary to re-focus. At the same time it is desirable to check the headlamp alignment as previously described.

The headlamp is correctly focused when the reflected rays of light are almost parallel and when the beam, projected upon a wall 30 to 40 ft from the machine, illuminates brightly a circular area of minimum diameter. The filament for the main driving light should be as near as possible to the focal point of the reflector in order to obtain a parallel beam. If the filament is positioned in front of the focal point, a converging beam (with dark centre portion) results. If, on the other hand, the filament is positioned behind the focal point, a diverging beam is obtained.

Both converging and diverging beams are highly undesirable as they illuminate the road poorly and are liable to dazzle other road users. Adjust the focus of the headlamp immediately if its beam is not uniform, is of short range, and has a dark centre. In order to focus the headlamp it is obviously necessary to move the main bulb backwards or forwards on the reflector axis according to whether the beam is converging or diverging respectively.

How To Focus DU-42 Headlamp. You should take your machine to a level stretch of road and focus the headlamp against a wall some distance (say about 40 ft) from the machine. The lamp front and reflector must first be removed. To do this, release the spring fixing clip (see Fig. 58) which secures the base of the lamp front and pull the latter outwards. As the lamp front and reflector come away together, free the top tag of the lamp front

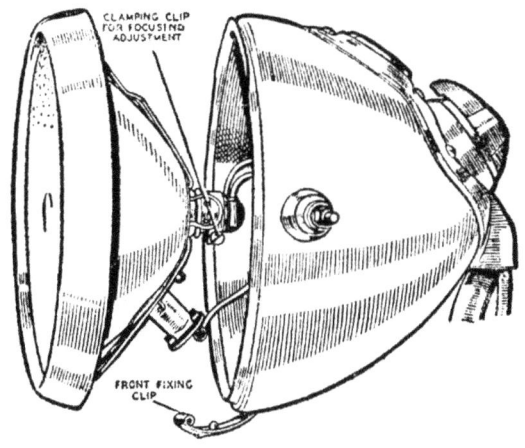

FIG. 58. FOCUSING ADJUSTMENT ON LUCAS DU-42 HEADLAMP

The lamp front and reflector are shown detached from the lamp body to reveal the clamping clip, which must be loosened to enable the bulb-holder to be moved for focusing

from the body of the lamp by lifting the lamp front slightly upwards.

The double-filament main bulb holder is adjustable in the plate fitted to the back of the reflector, and as may be seen in Fig. 58 there is a clamping clip for focusing adjustment. To focus the bulb, loosen the clamping screw on the clip and push the bulb-holder in or out of the clamping clip as required. Several focusing adjustments may be needed. After making each adjustment, replace the lamp front and reflector and test the beam for focus (see earlier paragraph). When the correct focus is obtained, tighten the screw on the bulb-holder clamping clip firmly.

When fitting the lamp front and reflector, first locate the top tag in the slot of the lamp body and then press home the lamp front towards the body. Finally, fasten the lamp front by means of the spring fixing clip at the base of the lamp.

Renewing Lucas Bulbs. If a bulb "goes west," fit a bulb of the correct type. Most large garages and accessory dealers stock genuine Lucas bulbs, which are all specially tested to check that the filament is correctly positioned to give maximum results *with Lucas reflectors*. It is advisable not to wait till bulbs actually burn-out but to renew them after long service. This avoids the risk of incorrect focusing caused by sagging of the filaments which sometimes occurs after extensive use.

Lucas bulbs have their metal caps marked with a number for identification purposes and it is important when renewing a bulb to see that it has the correct number on its cap. The number of the headlamp double-filament main bulb is 70 (180, coil ignition with E3H or E3AR dynamo); and that of the headlamp pilot, sidecar, and rear lamp bulbs, 200. The number 70 bulb is 6V., 24/24W. The number 180 is 6V., 18/18W. The number 200 bulb is 6V., 3W.

The headlamp main and pilot bulbs are fitted in holders attached to the plate secured to the rear of the reflector by two spring wires. To remove the plate, complete with the two holders and bulbs, it is only necessary to spring the two wires outwards until they are clear of the plate.

To remove the headlamp main bulb or pilot bulb from its holder, it is only necessary to release the bayonet fixing and withdraw the bulb.

It is essential when fitting a new main bulb to see that it is the correct way round, i.e. with the dipped beam filament *above* the centre filament. The word "Top" is etched on Lucas main bulbs to indicate the correct position in the bulb holder. After fitting a new main bulb it is advisable to check the focus of the headlamp (see page 124).

How to Remove Reflector (DU-42 Headlamp). Remove the four spring clips that secure the reflector and glass to the headlamp front and detach the reflector, the cork packing strip between the reflector and glass, and the glass itself.

To assemble the reflector and glass, the following procedure is necessary. First position the glass in the lamp front. Next, fit the cork packing strip to the reflector edge by pressing it into the pins which are integral with the lamp front. Then place the reflector assembly (complete with bulb holders) on top of the glass. Make sure that the top of the reflector registers with the top of the lamp front. Finally, replace the four spring clips so that they are about equally spaced.

The Lucas Ammeter. This centre-zero instrument, mounted on the Lucas DU-42 headlamp, shows a charge on one side of the dial and a discharge on the other side. Its purpose is to indicate the amount of current flowing to or from the battery.

For instance, if the dynamo output is 3 amp. at a certain speed, and the headlamp pilot bulb and rear lamp are switched on thereby

HINTS FOR COTTON OWNERS (1934 ON) 127

absorbing, say, 1 amp., then 2 amp. remain for charging the battery and the ammeter consequently indicates 2 amp.

When the engine is ticking over slowly, the dynamo does not

Fig. 59. Withdrawing Bulb Holder and Housing from Lucas MT110 Rear Lamp

rotate fast enough to charge the battery and the ammeter reading is zero; if the lamps are on, a discharge reading is, therefore, shown.

The Lucas MT110 Rear Lamp. As may be seen in Fig. 59, the portion of the MT110 rear lamp carrying the red glass is let into a

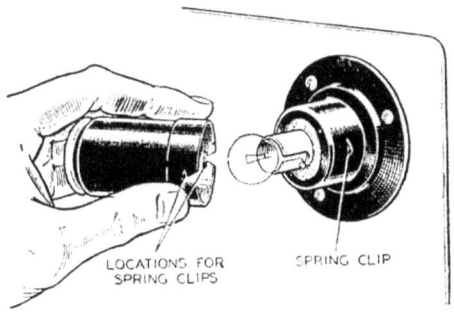

Fig. 60. Removing Lamp Front from Lucas MT111 Rear Lamp

circular hole in the rear number plate. To prevent vibration, the bulb holder (shown detached) is mounted on a rubber diaphragm. To remove the bulb-holder housing, turn it *anti-clockwise* slightly so as to release the bayonet fixing, and then withdraw.

For correct bulb replacement, see page 126. To replace the bulb-holder housing, engage the bayonet fixing and then turn the housing *clockwise* until it is firmly clipped into position.

The Lucas MT111 Rear Lamp. As may be seen in Fig. 60, with this lamp the lamp front, i.e. the portion carrying the red glass, is detachable from the body of the lamp carrying the bulb holder.

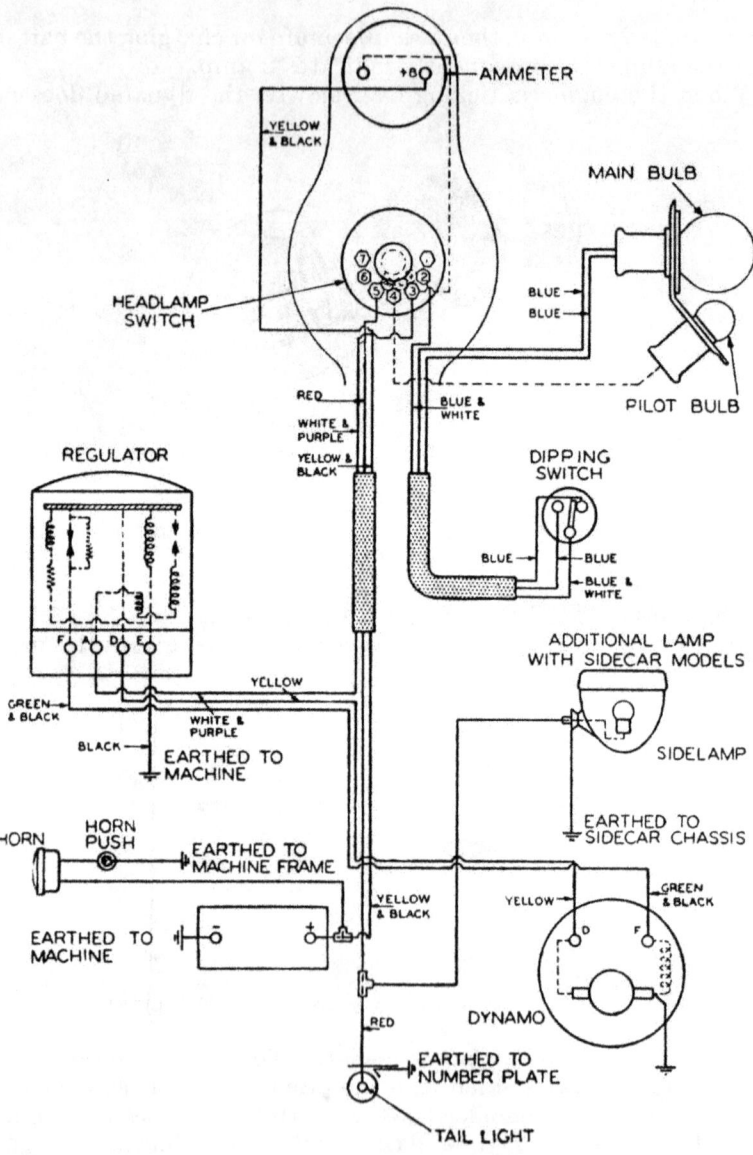

FIG. 61. WIRING DIAGRAM FOR LUCAS "MAGDYNO" LIGHTING EQUIPMENT WITHOUT INSTRUMENT PANEL, WITH COMPENSATED VOLTAGE CONTROL (1937 ONWARDS)
All internal connexions are shown dotted

HINTS FOR COTTON OWNERS (1934 ON)

The lamp body is secured by three screws to the rear number plate, and to remove the portion carrying the red glass, give it a half turn *anti-clockwise*.

To replace the lamp front, engage the locations for the spring clips with the two spring clips on the body of the lamp, and push home until firmly secured.

How to Clean Lucas Lamps. It is best to clean ebony black surfaces with a good type of car polish. Chromium-plated surfaces do not tarnish and these can be wiped over occasionally with a damp cloth to remove dust or dirt. Be careful when handling a reflector not to scratch it accidentally, and on *no* account use any metal polish.

All Lucas reflectors have a transparent protective covering and it is possible to clean this readily without any risk of spoiling the actual reflector surface. It is best to use a clean, dry, soft cloth, or else a chamois leather to polish the reflector covering. No other treatment is desirable.

CHAPTER VIII

J.A.P. ENGINED MOTOR-CYCLES

ALTHOUGH one main purpose of this handbook is to deal with the actual maintenance of J.A.P. engines, the author feels that a brief description of all current and recent motor-cycles embodying J.A.P. engines will be of interest, especially to those contemplating the purchase of new mounts. In this chapter reference

FIG. 62. MODERN IN CONCEPTION AND PERFORMANCE—
THE 500 c.c. O.H.V. "HIGH CAMSHAFT" COTTON—
MODEL 25/SPECIAL

The machine illustrated is typical of the Cotton breed which is renowned for stability and good performance. All engines are carefully run-in by the makers and installed in the well-known triangulated frame. Burman gearboxes and Lucas "Magdyno" lighting are fitted on the four-stroke Cotton models. The 250 c.c. S.V. model, however, has Miller coil ignition and lighting. Dowty "Oleomatic" front forks are optional

is made not only to machines powered with single-cylinder S.V. and O.H.V. engines, and S.V. Vee-twin engines, but also to a 1948-50 model having the 494 c.c. S.V. vertical twin engine.

The Cotton Range. Nine attractive single-cylinder models are continued for 1952. All 1952 single-cylinder models are very similar to the corresponding 1951 models. The 1952 range of single-cylinder models comprises: a lightweight, but decidedly "peppy" 122 c.c. two-stroke model, with Villiers two-port engine; a handy 250 c.c. side-valve mount; a powerful 600 c.c. side-valve model, suitable for solo or sidecar work; and six speedy and rakish looking overhead-valve machines. These six O.H.V. models are grouped into 250 c.c., 350 c.c., 500 c.c. De Luxe

J.A.P. ENGINED MOTOR-CYCLES

models and Special models having the same engine capacities. The engine fitted to the 500 c.c. O.H.V. De Luxe model is illustrated in Fig. 34. The three O.H.V. Special models, one of which is shown in Fig. 62, have "high camshaft" engines of the type shown in Fig. 17.

Full details of the 1951-2 Cotton models can be had on application to The Cotton Motor Co., of Gloucester.

FIG. 63. AN ATTRACTIVE S.V. VERTICAL TWIN—THE 500 C.C. A.J.W. "GREY FOX"

This 1948-50 spring frame modern "Fox" had a 494 c.c. S.V. J.A.P. engine, and struck a new note in motor-cycle design. Many desirable features are incorporated, including a cradle frame, rear springing, telescopic front forks, etc. For view of transmission side, see page 95

(*By courtesy of " The Motor Cycle "*)

The 1950 A.J.W. Range. For 1950 the makers of the A.J.W. motor-cycles concentrated only on the production of the A.J.W. "Grey Fox" and the "Speed Fox." The "Grey Fox" is a most interesting machine which was originally introduced in 1948. The machine (see Fig. 63) embodies the 494 c.c. S.V. vertical twin J.A.P. engine shown in Figs. 35 and 36. The "Grey Fox" besides being a real luxury machine, has an excellent all-round performance. Its full throttle speed on the level is about 75 m.p.h. It is not a thirsty mount, fuel and oil consumptions averaging for normal touring approximately 75 m.p.g. and 3000 m.p.g. respectively.

The "Speed Fox" is a special track mount powered with the famous 500 c.c. speedway J.A.P. engine. It has, of course, magneto ignition and is not intended for normal road use.

The 1948-50 "Grey Fox." This has an exciting specification, and it may be mentioned that the vertical twin engine and the gearbox can be removed and assembled *as one unit* in the new cradle frame. This frame is of the duplex type, incorporates *rear springing*, and is welded up according to the stresses involved. Some parts are fusion welded and some are made up with nickel bronze.

FIG. 64. IDEAL FOR THE FAMILY MAN—THE 1949 750 C.C. DE LUXE ZENITH BIG TWIN

With its powerful engine, this dual-purpose model is suitable for fast long distance solo work, or will transport the family anywhere without "fuss." Owing to its flexible engine, it is a nice machine to handle in traffic. Druidscopic forks were fitted in 1950

(*By courtesy of "The Motor Cycle"*)

Dowty "Oleomatic" front forks of the telescopic type and A.J.W. rear springing cushion all road bumps. Comfort as well as high performance have been very carefully considered by the makers, and a Lycett pan seat with back rest is included.

The "Grey Fox" should appeal to young "sporty" riders as well as to those who are "not so young," especially having regard to the easy starting and comfort provided. As regards reliability, it may be stated that a prototype "Grey Fox" has travelled some 6000 miles before tappet adjustment became remotely desirable!

The "Grey Fox" specification includes: a streamlined $2\frac{1}{4}$ gal. petrol tank; an Amal two-lever semi-automatic carburettor with special Burgess air cleaner; automatic ignition advance; vernier-valve timing; Burgess silencers; clean handlebars with only two levers and twist-grip throttle; a Burman or Albion four-speed gearbox (bolted up into a unit with the engine), provided with foot gear-change; a multi-plate Ferodo insert clutch with enclosed clutch operating mechanism; a folding kick-starter; a primary chain running in an oil-bath and provided with cam adjustment for tension.

Also included in the specification are: Smiths 120 m.p.h. speedometer; wheels fitted with non-adjustable journal bearings and 3·50 in. × 19 in. "Universal" Dunlop tyres; tommy-bar operation of rear wheel spindle nuts; rear mudguard with detachable tail piece; 7 in. diameter brakes with finger adjustment, front and rear; footrests adjustable for position and designed to fold on acute impact; a low lift centre spring-up stand; Lucas dyno-distributor unit (with C.V.C.) for coil ignition and lighting; a Lucas PUW7E battery; a 6½ in. Lucas MU-42 headlamp; a Lucas MT211 rear lamp; and a Lucas Altette horn.

Concerning A.J.W. Motor-cycles. The production of A.J.W. motor-cycles was discontinued after 1950 and A.J.W. Motor Cycles, Ltd., went into liquidation. However, J. O. Ball (A.J.W. Motor Cycles) of West Row, Wimborne, Dorset continues to make A.J.W. racing machines to order, can supply spares for all models, and specializes in A.J.W. repairs and overhauls.

1949-50 Zenith Big Twin. This dual-purpose machine should interest solo and sidecar riders, especially the latter. The machine is similar to the 1948 version, plus improvements, and its power unit is the well proved 747 c.c. side-valve Vee-twin J.A.P. engine having a bore and stroke of 70 mm. × 97 mm. The engine has wet sump lubrication with an adjustable Pilgrim pump, and roller bearings are provided for the big-end and main bearings. A special Amal carburettor is specified, and ignition and lighting are by a Lucas "Magdyno" with C.V.C. Other features of a well-planned specification include: a heavyweight Burman four-speed gearbox with foot control and enclosed clutch, polished aluminium oil-bath chain case for front chain, engine shaft shock absorber, Druid girder type or Druidscopic front forks (not illustrated), Zenith full duplex cradle frame of great strength, fully adjustable handlebars, and a Lycett saddle.

Dunlop tyres are fitted to both wheels which have taper roller bearings. The front tyre dimensions are 3·25 in. × 19 in., and the rear tyre dimensions 4·00 in. × 18 in. To facilitate tyre repairs, the rear mudguard has a readily detachable tail piece. The powerful internal expanding brakes are of 7 in. diameter.

The petrol tank, which is fitted with a hinged filler cap, has a capacity of 3 gal. It is smartly finished with a panel in Zenith purple and black. The oil tank is of welded steel and holds 4 pints. Fig. 64 shows an off-side view of the 750 c.c. De Luxe Zenith. Its neat layout is very apparent.

Zenith motor-cycles are no longer manufactured, but those who require spares and service should contact Zenith Motor Cycles of

Kennington Cross, S.E.11, or the London Distributors, Writers, Ltd., of Kennington Cross, S.E.11.

Speedway Models. There are various speedway machines (such as the Excelsior, O.E.C.) available, but as this handbook is written mainly for owners of standard models designed for ordinary road use, details of these racing machines are not included. See page 141.

APPENDIX

MISCELLANEOUS NOTES

Hints on Tyre Repairs (Non-synthetic). Probably you have had some kind of experience in this matter and the author will only mention a few hints. Punctures are a rare occurrence nowadays, and if tyre pressures are kept correct it is very unlikely that you will often have occasion to open the repair outfit. Punctures can frequently be saved by occasional scrutiny of the treads and

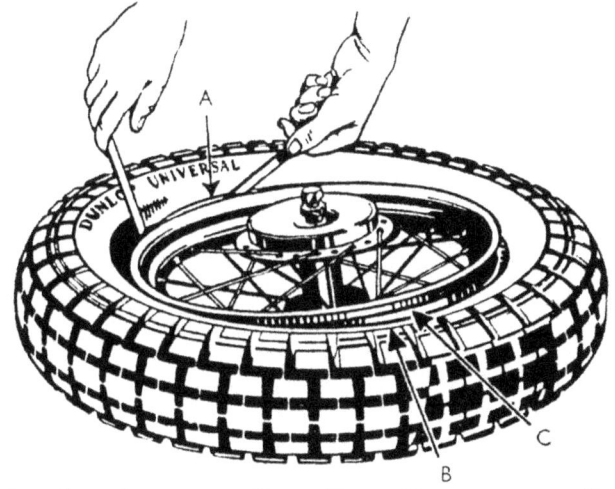

FIG. 65. THE SECRET OF EASY TYRE REMOVAL AND FITTING

Why do *some* motor-cyclists "struggle" helplessly with tyre covers? The reason is that a minority do not take into account the fact that wire beads are *inextensible*. It is essential to push the cover bead at *B* off the rim shoulder down into the well *C* before attempting to lever the cover bead at *A* over the rim flange

(*By courtesy of Dunlop Rubber Co., Ltd.*)

digging out with a small knife any flints or stones embedded in the rubber. When removing a cover, always begin *well away from the valve* and use the tyre levers firmly but gently. Use autovulcanizing type patches such as the Dunlop "Vulcafix." Apply the solution to the *tube only*. Test the tube afterwards if possible by partially inflating it and immersing it in a basin of water. Before refitting, dab it liberally with french chalk, and when replacing the cover see that the valve is pushed squarely home. Slight inflation will often assist refitting of the cover, the wire edges of which must be pushed right down into the well of the well-base rim (see Fig. 65).

Repairing GR-S Synthetic Tubes. Synthetic tubes made during and immediately after the war may be identified by means of a 1 in. diameter red disk close to the valve, or alternatively by a red stripe round the base of the tube. For the repair of such tubes good quality repair material of the same type as for pure rubber tubes should be used.

Although it is preferable to vulcanize all tube injuries, it is possible to make a satisfactory emergency repair of nail holes and small injuries up to $\frac{1}{4}$ in. by using an auto-vulcanizing type patch, such as the Dunlop "Vulcafix." The following procedure is recommended by the Dunlop Rubber Co. for repairing GR-S tubes.

Roughen the surface round the injury for an area slightly larger than the patch to be used. Employ a wire brush or sandpaper to remove surface glaze, and rub off all dust. Avoid making any deep scratches which may subsequently develop into splits. Now choose a suitable patch which should be of not less than 1$\frac{1}{2}$ in. diameter. Detach its glazed linen backing and apply one coat of solution to *the tube only.* Allow the solution to dry thoroughly and then apply the patch, pressing it down firmly. Dust the tube thoroughly in the vicinity of the patch with french chalk to prevent the tube or patch adhering to the cover. Where the cover is completely removed, dust the inside thoroughly with chalk before refitting it. If the tube injury exceeds about $\frac{1}{4}$ in., it is the best policy to take the tube to a competent repairer and have it vulcanized.

When fitting a GR-S synthetic tube to a cover, it is advisable to apply a frothy solution of soap and water liberally around the entire base of the tube, extending upwards between the tyre beads and the tube itself for at least 2 in. on both sides. Apply the soap solution also to the bottom and outside of the tyre beads. Avoid allowing the solution to run into the crown of the tyre. The strength of the solution should be such that it feels slippery on rubbing the fingers together. If soap solution is not to hand, use french chalk instead. It is advisable to inflate the tube very slightly *before* attempting to lever the cover home.

Before inflating the tube after levering the cover home, make sure that the tyre beads are clear of the well of the rim all the way round. Inflate the tube gradually until the beads are fully seated. Then deflate the tube completely and re-inflate to the correct pressure.

Burman Gearbox Lubrication. Burman gearboxes are fitted to most J.A.P.-engined motor-cycles, including Cottons, and the following points should be noted in addition to the lubrication

APPENDIX 137

instructions given on page 111 in the Cotton section. Where a speedometer drive is fitted to the gearbox, occasionally remove and grease the small spindle housed in the clutch lever bracket (on three-speed and Model H type gearboxes), or in the kick-starter case cover (on four-speed Models C and BA gearboxes). When replacing the clutch lever bracket, pack this also with grease. Occasionally grease the foot-change mechanism also. Suitable greases for Burman gearbox lubrication are specified on page 112.

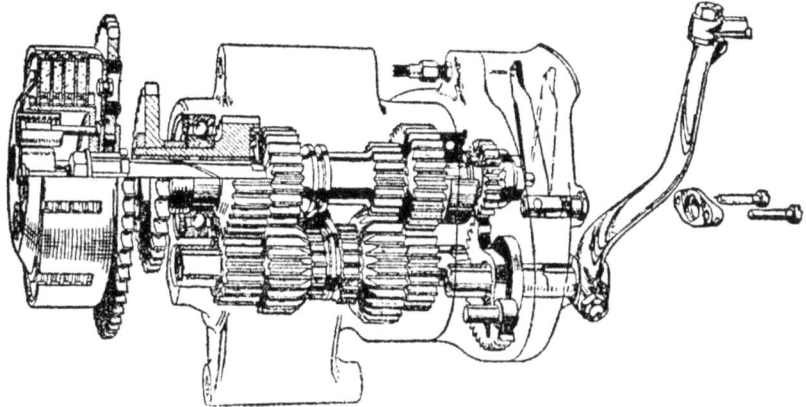

FIG. 66. SHOWING DETAILS OF BURMAN FOUR-SPEED GEARBOX AND MULTI-PLATE CLUTCH

The gearbox illustrated has enclosed kick-starter, and clutch mechanism, and is fitted to the Cotton, Zenith, etc. On the A.J.W. "Grey Fox" the casing is different. For clutch details, see Figs. 46, 47

In this connexion it should be noted that Shell Motor Grease Soft can be used as an alternative to Shell Retinax.

Dismantling Burman Three-speed Gearbox (Types R, T, W, G). First remove the clutch lever bracket and kick-starter. Having removed these items, unscrew the nut (R.H. thread) on the kick-starter end of the mainshaft. To facilitate removing the nut, engage second gear and lock the rear wheel by applying the brake. Next withdraw the ratchets with the fingers, remove the nuts holding the kick-starter case in position, and draw off the case. Now withdraw together the mainshaft and clutch. Then unscrew the pawl spring plug located beneath the gearbox (except on the G type box where it is on the L.H. side) and remove the gears themselves.

Assembling Burman Three-speed Gearbox. Assembly procedure is quite straightforward, but a few points should be noted. Mesh the two sliding gears with each other by means of the flanges, and see that the operating block is fitted in the groove on the sliding gear of the mainshaft and is connected to the peg on the bell-crank lever. If the screw on the left-hand side of the gearbox has been loosened or removed, make certain that it is firmly retightened. Never remove this screw except when dismantling the gearbox.

Dismantling Burman Four-speed Gearbox (Types H, BA, G, A). The Burman type H gearbox is of similar design to the three-speed type, and the instructions previously given for dismantling the three-speed type apply also in general to the four-speed type H gearboxes.

To dismantle type BA, G, A gearboxes, remove the outer lever and the nuts around the cover of the kick-starter case. It is not necessary to dismantle the actual kick-starter. After removing the cover, unscrew the nut on the mainshaft and also the small nuts which hold the kick-starter case in position. Now remove the pawl spring and withdraw the gear assembly.

FIG. 67. THE A.G.I. "EASILIFT" MOTOR-CYCLE REPAIR STAND

Assembling Burman Four-speed Gearbox. When assembling the type H gearbox, fit the layshaft assembly first, with the two sliding members together. Before fitting the mainshaft, replace the mainshaft sliding gear so as to clamp the flanges of the layshaft sliding gears.

To assemble the type BA, G, A gearboxes, follow the reverse order of dismantling. Use some thick grease to hold the camshaft rollers in place while replacing the kick-starter case. Make sure that the "O" markings on the small gear on the end of the camshaft and the gear sector coincide.

Burman Clutch Adjustment. Always maintain $\frac{1}{32}$ in. clearance between the end of the push-rod and the ball in the clutch lever. Keep the spring adjusting nuts tightened so as to be flush with the plate carrying the adjusting springs.

Dismantling Burman Foot Gear Change. On the three-speed gearboxes and the H type four-speed gearboxes, remove the kick-starter case, when the gear-change mechanism can be readily dismantled.

On other types of four-speed gearboxes, unscrew the six nuts which secure the cover, remove the cover and dismantle the mechanism thereby exposed.

APPENDIX

Spares, Tools, and Accessories. Owners of J.A.P. engined machines can obtain spares and tools for engine replacements and overhaul direct from J. A. Prestwich & Co., Ltd., of Tottenham, N.17 (Tot. 3701); from the motor-cycle makers, or from J.A.P. spares stockists. Writers, Ltd., of Kennington Cross, S.E.11, are official spares and tools stockists in the London area. This firm (distributors for the Zenith) also supply spares for Amal carburettors and Burman and Sturmey-Archer gearboxes. In addition they undertake repairs, welding, straightening, and enamelling. Another firm which specializes on a big scale in J.A.P. spares and undertakes all types of engine overhauls and reconditioning, including cylinder grinding and sleeving, is Frank Leach

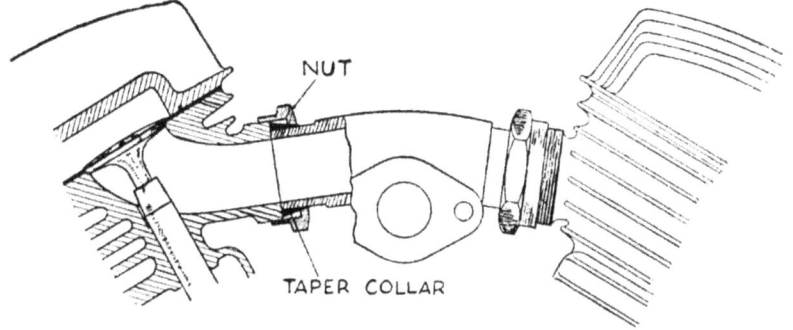

FIG. 68. DETAILS OF INDUCTION PIPE CONNEXION ON J.A.P. VEE-TWIN ENGINES

Motors, Ltd., of York Street, Leeds, 9. Special J.A.P. racing fuel can be obtained from this firm, also racing engines and J.A.P. engines for industrial use. Racing engines, spares for racing engines, and tyres can also be obtained from Alec. Jackson, of 1006 Harrow Road, London, N.W.10.

The author would also draw the reader's attention to five large accessory firms who can supply an immense variety of motor-cycle spares, tyres, accessories, tools, clothing, and sundry equipment. These firms (with branches throughout the U.K.) are: The Halford Cycle Co., Ltd.; George Grose, Ltd.; Turner's Stores; Marble Arch Motor Supplies, Ltd.; and James Grose, Ltd.

Overhauling in Comfort. Motor-cyclists who like to work on their engines and machines in maximum comfort, without unnecessary bending and kneeling, are reminded of an excellent and reasonably priced repair stand known as the A.G.I. "Easilift," illustrated in Fig. 67. This stand is readily operated by hand and will raise the heaviest motor-cycle to a comfortable working height with very little effort. It occupies a floor space of 7ft. 6 in. × 18 in. and is obtainable through motor-cycle dealers.

To Secure Even Running on Vee Twins. With twin-cylinder J.A.P. engines it is important, especially having regard to smooth slow-running and even firing, to see that *both* sparking plugs have precisely the *same* gap, and that the valve springs on both cylinders have the same degree of tension. The contact-breaker gap must also be the same for both cylinders. In addition, there must be no air leaks in the induction system. A badly worn inlet valve

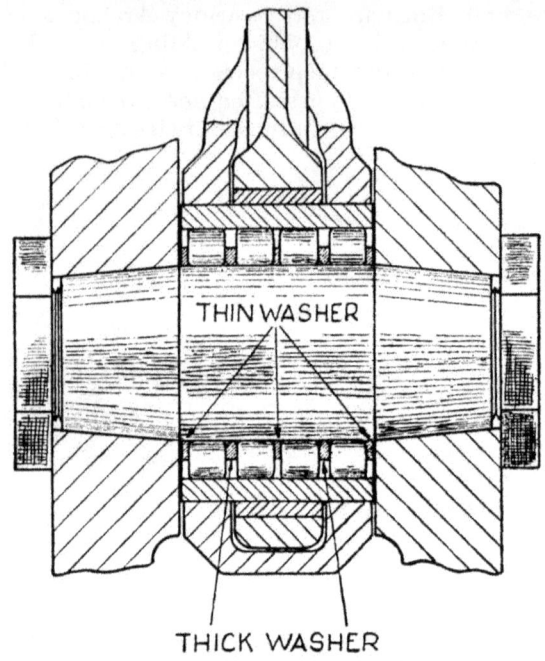

FIG. 69. BIG-END ASSEMBLY USED ON 1100 C.C. ENGINES

guide in one cylinder or a leak at an induction pipe connexion may produce considerable irregularity in running.

The J.A.P. method of attaching the induction pipe to the inlet ports of Vee type twin-cylinder engines is shown in Fig. 68. As may be observed, the pipe is of uniform diameter throughout its length and at each end of the pipe there is a taper collar which is a sliding fit on the pipe. Each union nut has an internal taper which corresponds to the taper on the taper collar, or ferrule. Thus when the union nut is screwed to the inlet port, it tightens the ferrule down on to the pipe and secures an air-tight joint, and at the same time allows for expansion of the cylinder.

When fitting the induction pipe, make sure that the pipe, ferrules, and union nuts are clean, and tighten down both union nuts evenly and firmly.

APPENDIX 141

Big-end Assembly on Vee Twins. On all Vee twin engines there is a forked connecting-rod, and also a plain rod whose big-end fits in the centre of the forked rod. The forked rod reciprocates in No. 2 (the front) cylinder.

The big-end is of the roller type, four rows of rollers being provided. These rollers are separated by steel washers which must be arranged as shown in Fig. 69. In the event of the big-end assembly being dismantled, see that the washers are correctly disposed on assembly.

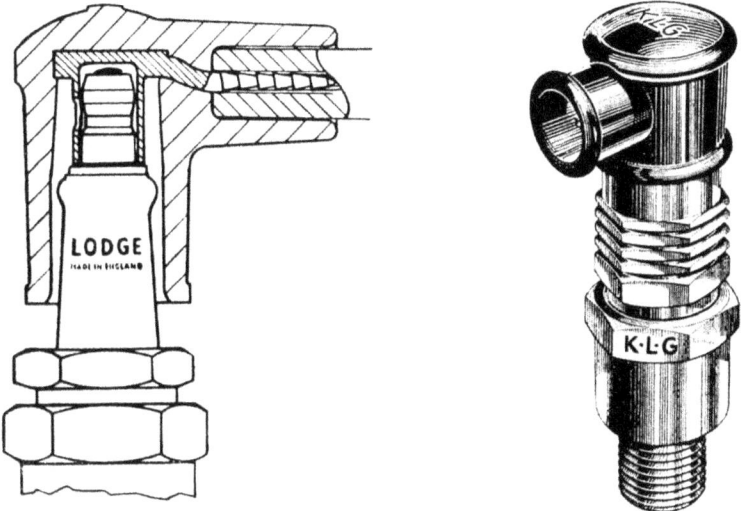

FIG. 70. WEATHERPROOF TERMINAL COVER AND SPARKING PLUG
On the left is shown the Lodge weatherproof terminal cover, and on the right the excellent K.L.G. watertight plug

Concerning J.A.P. Racing Engines. Racing engines should *not* be run at normal touring speeds. They develop their maximum power output at very high r.p.m., and consequently have a racing timing gear and reciprocating parts which are lighter than those fitted on standard type engines. In other respects the racing engines do not differ appreciably from the standard type, and the appropriate instructions given in this handbook apply.

To obtain the best results from J.A.P. racing engines, always fit a good racing sparking plug such as the Lodge R49 or R51. Reduce friction throughout the engine and motor-cycle parts as far as possible and choose the right gear ratios for the particular job contemplated. Also see that the compression ratio of the engine is correct, according to the fuel to be used.

If the compression ratio is raised above standard, make quite sure that there is a full $\frac{5}{32}$ in. clearance between the valve heads and the crown of the piston, otherwise a most disastrous collision is inevitable! Various J.A.P. pistons are obtainable for running on petrol-benzole and alcohol fuels and the compression ratio can also be reduced to suit a petrol-benzol mixture (50 per cent pure benzol).

On O.H.V. racing engines various washers are obtainable for insertion beneath the cylinder base in order to reduce the C.R. Unless suitable washers are fitted, a proper racing fuel *must* be employed in order to prevent detonation. Where the maximum number of washers is inserted, the cylinder barrel is raised $\frac{5}{32}$ in. This, by the way, entails the fitting of extra long push-rods.

Weatherproof Sparking Plugs. Owners of J.A.P. engined motorcycles who do much all weather riding are strongly advised to fit a weatherproof plug terminal or else a watertight plug. Fig. 70 shows the Lodge weatherproof and shockproof terminal cover

VALVE AND IGNITION TIMINGS FOR 1949-50 J.A.P. ENGINES

Type of Engine	Inlet		Exhaust		Ignition
	Opens Before T.D.C.	Closes After B.D.C.	Opens Before B.D.C.	Closes After T.D.C.	Advance Before T.D.C.
350 c.c. S.V. (wet sump)	15°	50°	50°	20°	40°
350° c.c. S.V. (dry sump)	10°	50°	50°	20°	40°
350° c.c. O.H.V. (grass track)	44°	62°	65°	34°	37°
500 c.c. O.H.V. (speedway)	44°	62°	65°	34°	37°
750 c.c. S.V. (vee twin)	18°	45°	60°	25°	40°
1100 c.c. Mk. 1 (racing)	55°	74°	74°	42°	38°

which can be readily fitted and does not shake loose. It is thoroughly insulated and costs 1s. 6d. A K.L.G. terminal cover is also obtainable for 2s.

A K.L.G. watertight sparking plug is shown in Fig. 70 (right-hand illustration). Based on aircraft experience, the gland nut has an extension in the form of a metal sleeve (see Fig. 70) designed to give a tight snap-on fit, with a specially toughened moulded cap. The sleeve protects the insulator completely, and fins are provided to disperse excessive heat. The body of the plug is of rust resistant steel. The complete plug is thoroughly waterproof, dustproof, and oilproof.

APPENDIX 143

Watertight 18 mm. and 14 mm. K.L.G. plugs cost 8s. 6d. each. The correct type numbers for these plugs are those given on page 52, preceded by the letter "W" (e.g. WF70, etc.).

Valve and Ignition Timings (1949-50). The accompanying table shows in degrees of crankshaft rotation the correct valve timings for all 1949-50 J.A.P. four-stroke engines. The correct ignition timings are also indicated. The 350 c.c. S.V. engine with *sump* lubrication (the second referred to in the table) is one used exclusively for industrial purposes, such as lawn mowers. The timings for the 494 c.c. S.V. vertical twin engine are not included in the Table, as these are given on pages 74 and 75.

General instructions on the procedure for timing the ignition and valves are given on pages 53-63.

Retiming Ignition (Miller DH1 Dynamo). On coil ignition models having a Miller DH1 dynamo (1950-2, 250 c.c. S.V. Cottons) it is *not* possible to rectify the moment of contact opening at the contact-breaker as in the case of coil ignition models with other types of Miller dynamos or Lucas dynamos having the contacts operated by a central cam (which can be released and moved). On Miller DH1 dynamo models it is necessary to release the driving gear and proceed as for Lucas "Magdyno" models (see page 56).

INDEX

Accessory firms, 139
Air filter, 69, 92
A.J.W.—
  "Grey Fox," 88, 132
  machines (1934-9), 77-87
  Motor Cycles, Ltd., 133
Albion gearbox, 83, 93, 100
Amal carburettor, 41-4
Ammeter, 121, 126

Battery, care of, 80, 102, 110, 121
Belt drive, dynamo, 79
"Best" pump, 10
Bevel-driven magneto, 60
Big-end bearing, 64, 65, 141
Bowden carburettor—
  action of, 44, 108
  tuning, 46
Brake—
  adjustment, 97
  lubrication, 87, 94
  shoes, 98
"Break," adjusting, 56
Bulbs, 83, 103, 111, 125
Burgess—
  air filter, 92
  silencers, 83, 92
Burman—
  clutch, 98, 112, 138
  gearbox, 93, 111, 136-8

Carburettor, 38-47, 69, 78, 92, 107
Charging battery, 81, 103, 121-3
Chromium, cleaning, 96
Circlips, removing, 21, 72
Cleaning—
  engine, 30, 91
  machine, 95-6, 113
  piston rings, 23
Clutch, 84, 98, 112, 138
Coil ignition, 57, 74, 109
Combustion chamber, 25
Commutator, 12, 79, 87, 102, 119
Contact-breaker, 48, 68, 78, 109

Contacts, cleaning, 51
Controls, 69, 77, 90, 107-9
Cork inserts, 100
Cotton machines, 107-31
Crankcase, flushing out, 12, 68, 107
C.V.C., 102, 120
Cylinder—
  decarbonizing, 24, 73
  removing, 20, 72, 92
  replacing, 30, 73
  wear, 63

Decarbonizing—
  A.J.W., 83, 92
  Cotton, 91, 111
  piston, cylinder, 24, 73
Degree disk, 57
"Dipper" lubrication, 66
Dip-stick, 67, 91
Dismantling—
  overhead-valve engines, 16, 19
  side-valve engines, 15, 70
Dowty "Oleomatic" front forks, 94, 114-19
Dry sump system, 1
Dynamo maintenance, 12, 13, 68, 77, 79, 107
Dyno-distributor unit, 68, 75, 102, 105

Enamelled parts, cleaning, 96
End play, rocker, 36
Engine—
  oils, 1, 67
  pinion, removing, 60
  removing, 104, 111
Exhaust valve lifter adjustment, 37

Filter, cleaning, 6, 12, 107
Float chamber needle, defective, 40
Flooding carburettor, 69, 90, 108-9
Flushing—
  crankcase, 12, 68, 107
  gearbox, 93

INDEX

Focusing headlamp, 81-3, 103, 124
Footrest adjustment, 89
Front forks—
  girder, 86, 114
  "Oleomatic," 94, 114-18

GAITERS, A.J.W., cleaning, 96
Gap—
  contact-breaker, 50, 68, 79, 109
  piston ring, 24, 72
  sparking plug, 47, 68, 92, 109
Gear control adjustment, 84
Generator chain, 110
"Grey Fox," 88-106, 132
Grinding-in valves, 28, 73
Grooves, ring, cleaning, 23
Gudgeon-pin, removing, 20, 72

HANDLEBAR adjustment, 89
Headlamps, 81-3, 102-3, 118, 123-6
"High camshaft" engines, 8, 19, 35, 130
Hub bearings, 94, 98, 113

IGNITION—
  system, maintenance of, 47-53, 68, 77-8, 92, 102, 107, 109-10
  timing, 53-7, 74, 79, 92, 109
Induction pipe, 140
Inflating "Oleomatic" forks, 114

J.A.P.—
  oil-box, 3
  pump, 2, 7
  rings, 63, 72
  valve and ignition timings, 55, 74, 142, 143
  valve grinding tool, 28

LAMPS, cleaning, 129
Licences, 88
Lighting switch positions, 103, 124
Loading indicators, fork, 114
Lubrication—
  cycle parts, 83-7, 92-5, 111-16
  engine, 1-13, 66-8, 77, 91, 107
Lucas lighting equipment, specification, 118

"MAGDYNO" lubrication, 13, 119
Magneto—
  chain, adjusting, 57
  lubrication, 12
  lubrication, 12
Mainshaft bearings, testing, 64
Miller dynamo, 79, 109

OIL—
  -bath chain case, 93, 105, 112
  -box, J.A.P., 3
  circulation, 2, 9, 66
  leakages, 7, 12, 94
Oils, engine, 1, 67
"Oleomatic" front forks, 94, 114-19
Overhead valve gear—
  lubrication, 5, 12
  re-assembling, 31

PETROL tank removal, 83, 104, 111
Pick-up, H.T., 52
Pilgrim pump, 9
Pillion passenger, 88
Piston—
  decarbonizing, 24, 73
  marking, 21, 72
  removing, 20, 72
  replacing, 30
  rings, removing, 21-3, 72
Pitted contacts, 51
"Pocketed" valves, 26
Preliminaries, legal, 88
Pressure gauge, tyre, 97
Primary chain, 84, 93, 100, 112
Priming "Best" pump, 10
Pump—
  adjustments, 9, 10
  troubles, 8, 11
Push-rods, removing, 16
"Python" gearbox, 83

RACING engines, 64, 139, 141
Rear lamps, 103, 127
Rear springing, A.J.W., 94, 96, 106
Repair stand, 139
Repairs, 139
Replenishment, oil, 1, 5, 9, 67, 77, 91, 107
Rich mixture, 38, 46
Rings—
  examining, 23, 63, 72
  removing, 21, 72

Rocker—
   adjustment, 33-7
   -arm, contact-breaker, 49
   -box—
      end play, 36
      removing, 16
Rotary valve, 3, 7
Running-in, 1, 69, 90

SADDLE adjustment, 113
Scraper, home-made, 23
Seats, valve, testing, 30
Secondary chain, 85, 94, 101, 112
Sight-feed glass filling up, 11
Slow-running, 42, 107, 140
Spares, 133, 139
Sparking plugs, 47-8, 68, 78, 92, 109
Speedometer, 87-8, 95, 113
Speedway models, 134
Spring—
   compressors, valve, 27
   link, fitting, 101
Starting—
   device, 108
   up, 41, 69, 78, 90, 107-9
Steering head, 86, 94, 101, 113-14
Stop, rear brake pedal, 97
Stuck piston rings, 22
Synthetic tubes, 136

TANK—
   oil, cleaning, 6, 12, 68, 107
   petrol, removing, 83, 104, 111
Tappets, adjusting, 33, 69
Telescopic forks, 94, 114-19
Terry ring remover, 22

Timing—
   case cover, removing, 60, 71
   chart, 55
   gears, worn, 61
   ignition, 53-7, 74
   rotary valve, 4
   valves, 59, 75-6, 142-3
Topping-up—
   battery, 81, 102, 105, 122
   "Oleomatic" forks, 94, 116
Transmission chains, 84, 85, 93, 100, 101, 112
Tyre—
   pressures, 86, 97, 113
   repairs, 135-6

VALVE—
   caps, removing, 14
   clearances, 33, 69, 92
   guides, testing, 28
   removal, 26-8, 73
   timing, 59, 75-6, 142-3
Vee-twin, 132
   big-end, 141
Vertical twin engine, 65-76

WEAK mixture, 39
Weatherproof sparking plugs, 142
Wet sump system, 8
Wheel—
   front, 85, 94, 98-105, 116
   rear, 85, 94, 98, 105, 113
Wiring diagram—
   Lucas, 128
   Miller, 82

ZENITH Big Twin, 133

AUTOBOOKS WORKSHOP MANUALS

ALFA ROMEO GIULIA 1300, 1600, 1750, 2000 1962-1978 WSM
BMW 1600 1966-1973 WSM
BMW 2000 & 2002 1966-1976 WSM
BMW 2500, 2800, 3.0 & 3.3 1968-1977 WSM
BMW 316, 320, 320i 1975-1977 WSM
BMW 518, 520, 520i 1973-1981 WSM
FIAT 1100, 1100D, 1100R & 1200 1957-1969 WSM
FIAT 124 1966-1974 WSM
FIAT 124 SPORT 1966-1975 WSM
FIAT 125 & 125 SPECIAL 1967-1973 WSM
FIAT 126, 126L, 126 DV, 126/650 & 126/650 DV 1972-1982 WSM
FIAT 127 SALOON, SPECIAL & SPORT, 900, 1050 1971-1981 WSM
FIAT 128 1969-1982 WSM
FIAT 1300, 1500 1961-1967 WSM
FIAT 131 MIRAFIORI 1975-1982 WSM
FIAT 132 1972-1982 WSM
FIAT 500 1957-1973 WSM
FIAT 600, 600D & MULTIPLA 1955-1969 WSM
FIAT 850 1964-1972 WSM
JAGUAR E-TYPE 1961-1972 WSM
JAGUAR MK 1, 2 1955-1969 WSM
JAGUAR S TYPE, 420 1963-1968 WSM
JAGUAR XK 120, 140, 150 MK 7, 8, 9 1948-1961 WSM
LAND ROVER 1, 2 1948-1961 WSM
MERCEDES-BENZ 190 1959-1968 WSM
MERCEDES-BENZ 220/8 1968-1972 WSM
MERCEDES-BENZ 220B 1959-1965 WSM
MERCEDES-BENZ 230 1963-1968 WSM
MERCEDES-BENZ 250 1968-1972 WSM
MERCEDES-BENZ 280 1968-1972 WSM
MG MIDGET TA-TF 1936-1955 WSM
MINI 1959-1980 WSM
MORRIS MINOR 1952-1971 WSM
PEUGEOT 404 1960-1975 WSM
PORSCHE 911 1964-1973 WSM
PORSCHE 911 1970-1977 WSM
RENAULT 16 1965-1979 WSM
RENAULT 8, 10, 1100 1962-1971 WSM
ROVER 3500, 3500S 1968-1976 WSM
SUNBEAM RAPIER, ALPINE 1955-1965 WSM
TRIUMPH SPITFIRE, GT6, VITESSE 1962-1968 WSM
TRIUMPH TR2, TR3, TR3A 1952-1962 WSM
TRIUMPH TR4, TR4A 1961-1967 WSM
VOLKSWAGEN BEETLE 1968-1977 WSM

VELOCEPRESS AUTOMOBILE BOOKS & MANUALS

ABARTH BUYERS GUIDE
AUSTIN-HEALEY 6-CYLINDER WSM
AUSTIN-HEALEY SPRITE & MG MIDGET 1958-1971 WSM
BMW 600 LIMOUSINE FACTORY WSM
BMW 600 LIMOUSINE OWNERS HAND BOOK & SERVICE MANUAL
BMW ISETTA FACTORY WSM
BOOK OF THE CARRERA PANAMERICANA - MEXICAN ROAD RACE
COMPLETE CATALOG OF JAPANESE MOTOR VEHICLES
CORVAIR 1960-1969 OWNERS WORKSHOP MANUAL
CORVETTE V8 1955-1962 OWNERS WORKSHOP MANUAL
DIALED IN - THE JAN OPPERMAN STORY
FERRARI 250/GT SERVICE AND MAINTENANCE
FERRARI 308 SERIES BUYER'S AND OWNER'S GUIDE
FERRARI BERLINETTA LUSSO
FERRARI BROCHURES AND SALES LITERATURE 1946-1967
FERRARI BROCHURES AND SALES LITERATURE 1968-1989
FERRARI GUIDE TO PERFORMANCE
FERRARI OPP, MAINTENANCE & SERVICE H/BOOKS 1948-1963
FERRARI OWNER'S HANDBOOK
FERRARI SERIAL NUMBERS PART I - ODD NUMBERS TO 21399
FERRARI SERIAL NUMBERS PART II - EVEN NUMBERS TO 1050
FERRARI SPYDER CALIFORNIA
FERRARI TUNING TIPS & MAINTENANCE TECHNIQUES
HENRY'S FABULOUS MODEL "A" FORD
HOW TO BUILD A FIBERGLASS CAR
HOW TO BUILD A RACING CAR
HOW TO RESTORE THE MODEL 'A' FORD
IF HEMINGWAY HAD WRITTEN A RACING NOVEL
JAGUAR E-TYPE 3.8 & 4.2 WSM
LE MANS 24 (THE BOOK THAT THE FILM WAS BASED ON)
MASERATI BROCHURES AND SALES LITERATURE
MASERATI OWNER'S HANDBOOK
METROPOLITAN FACTORY WSM
MGA & MGB OWNERS HANDBOOK & WSM
OBERT'S FIAT GUIDE
PERFORMANCE TUNING THE SUNBEAM TIGER
PORSCHE 356 1948-1965 WSM
PORSCHE 912 WSM
SOUPING THE VOLKSWAGEN
TRIUMPH TR2, TR3, TR4 1953-1965 WSM
TUNING FOR SPEED (P.E. IRVING)
VEDA ORR'S NEW REVISED HOT ROD PICTORIAL
VOLKSWAGEN TRANSPORTER, TRUCKS, STATION WAGONS WSM
VOLVO 1944-1968 ALL MODELS WSM
WEBER CARBURETORS (EMPHASIS ON ALFA & FIAT)

BROOKLANDS BOOKS & ROAD TEST PORTFOLIOS (RTP)

AC CARS 1904-2009
ALFA ROMEO 1920-1933 ROAD TEST PORTFOLIO
ALFA ROMEO 1934-1940 ROAD TEST PORTFOLIO
BRABHAM RALT HONDA THE RON TAURANAC STORY
BUGATTI TYPE 10 TO TYPE 40 ROAD TEST PORTFOLIO
BUGATTI TYPE 10 TO TYPE 251 ROAD TEST PORTFOLIO
BUGATTI TYPE 41 TO TYPE 55 ROAD TEST PORTFOLIO
BUGATTI TYPE 57 TO TYPE 251 ROAD TEST PORTFOLIO
DELAHAYE ROAD TEST PORTFOLIO
FERRARI ROAD CARS 1946-1956 ROAD TEST PORTFOLIO
FIAT 500 1936-1972 ROAD TEST PORTFOLIO
FIAT DINO ROAD TEST PORTFOLIO
HISPANO SUIZA ROAD TEST PORTFOLIO
HONDA ST1100/ST1300 PAN EUROPEAN 1990-2002 RTP
JAGUAR MK1 & MK2 ROAD TEST PORTFOLIO
LOTUS CORTINA ROAD TEST PORTFOLIO
MV AGUSTA F4 750 & 1000 1997-2007 ROAD TEST PORTFOLIO
TATRA CARS ROAD TEST PORTFOLIO

VELOCEPRESS MOTORCYCLE BOOKS & MANUALS

AJS SINGLES & TWINS 250cc THRU 1000cc 1932-1948 (BOOK OF)
AJS SINGLES 1955-65 350cc & 500cc (BOOK OF)
AJS SINGLES 1945-60 350cc & 500cc MODELS 16 & 18 (BOOK OF)
ARIEL 1939-1960 4 STROKE SINGLES (BOOK OF)
ARIEL LEADER & ARROW 1958-1964 (BOOK OF)
ARIEL MOTORCYCLES 1933-1951 WSM
ARIEL PREWAR MODELS 1932-1939 (BOOK OF)
BMW M/CYCLES R26 R27 (1956-1967) FACTORY WSM
BMW M/CYCLES R50 R50S R60 R69S (1955-1969) FACTORY WSM
BSA BANTAM (BOOK OF)
BSA ALL FOUR-STROKE SINGLES & V-TWINS 1936-1952 (BOOK OF)
BSA OHV & SV SINGLES - 250cc 1954-1970 (BOOK OF)
BSA OHV & SV SINGLES 1945-54 250-600cc (BOOK OF)
BSA OHV SINGLES 350 & 500cc 1955-1967 (BOOK OF)
BSA PRE-WAR MODELS TO 1939 (BOOK OF)
BSA TWINS 1948-1962 (BOOK OF)
BSA TWINS 1962-1969 (SECOND BOOK OF)
CATALOG OF BRITISH MOTORCYCLES (1951 MODELS)
DOUGLAS PRE-WAR ALL MODELS 1929-1939 (BOOK OF)
DOUGLAS POST-WAR ALL MODELS 1948-1957 FACTORY WSM
DUCATI 160cc, 250cc & 350cc OHC MODELS FACTORY WSM
HONDA 50 ALL MODELS UP TO 1970 INC MONKEY & TRAIL (BOOK OF)
HONDA 90 ALL MODELS UP TO 1966 (BOOK OF)
HONDA MOTORCYCLES 125-150 TWINS C/CS/CB/CA WSM
HONDA MOTORCYCLES 250-305 TWINS C/CS/CB WSM
HONDA MOTORCYCLES C100 SUPER CUB WSM
HONDA MOTORCYCLES C110 SPORT CUB 1962-1969 WSM
HONDA TWINS & SINGLES 50cc THRU 305cc 1960-1966 (BOOK OF)
HONDA TWINS ALL MODELS 125cc THRU 450cc UP TO 1968 (BOOK OF)
INDIAN PONYBIKE, BOY RACER & PAPOOSE ILL PARTS LIST & SALES LIT
J.A.P. ENGINES 1927-1952 & MOTORCYCLES 1934-1952 (BOOK OF)
LAMBRETTA ALL 125 & 150cc MODELS 1947-1957 (BOOK OF)
LAMBRETTA LI & TV MODELS 1957-1970 (SECOND BOOK OF)
MATCHLESS 350 & 500cc SINGLES 1945-1956 (BOOK OF)
MATCHLESS 350 & 500cc SINGLES 1955-1966 (BOOK OF)
NORTON 1932-1947 (BOOK OF)
NORTON 1938-1956 (BOOK OF)
NORTON DOMINATOR TWINS 1955-1965 (BOOK OF)
NORTON MODELS 19, 50 & ES2 1955-1963 (BOOK OF)
NORTON MOTORCYCLES 1957-1970 FACTORY WSM
NORTON PREWAR MODELS 1932-1939 (BOOK OF)
NSU QUICKLY ALL MODELS 1953-1963 (BOOK OF)
RALEIGH MOPEDS 1960-1969 (BOOK OF)
ROYAL ENFIELD SINGLES & V TWINS 1937-1953 (BOOK OF)
ROYAL ENFIELD SINGLES 1946-1962 (BOOK OF)
ROYAL ENFIELD 736cc INTERCEPTOR FACTORY WSM
ROYAL ENFIELD 250cc & 350cc SINGLES 1958-1966 (SECOND BOOK OF)
SUNBEAM MOTORCYCLES 1928-1939 (BOOK OF)
SUNBEAM S7 & S8 1946-1957 (BOOK OF)
SUZUKI 50cc & 80cc UP TO 1966 (BOOK OF)
SUZUKI T10 1963-1967 FACTORY WSM
SUZUKI T20 & T200 1965-1969 FACTORY WSM
TRIUMPH PRE-WAR MOTORCYCLE 1935-1939 (BOOK OF)
TRIUMPH MOTORCYCLES 1937-1951 WSM
TRIUMPH MOTORCYCLES 1945-1955 FACTORY WSM
TRIUMPH TWINS 1956-1969 (BOOK OF)
VELOCETTE ALL SINGLES & TWINS 1925-1970 (BOOK OF)
VESPA 1951-1961 (BOOK OF)
VESPA 125 & 150cc & GS MODELS 1955-1963 (SECOND BOOK OF)
VESPA 90, 125 & 150cc 1963-1972 (THIRD BOOK OF)
VESPA GS & SS 1955-1968 (BOOK OF)
VILLIERS ENGINE (BOOK OF)
VINCENT MOTORCYCLES 1935-1955 WSM

PLEASE VISIT OUR WEBSITE
www.VelocePress.com
FOR A DETAILED DESCRIPTION
OF ANY OF THESE TITLES

Please check our website:

www.VelocePress.com

for a complete up-to-date list of available titles

www.ingramcontent.com/pod-product-compliance
Lightning Source LLC
Chambersburg PA
CBHW070551170426
43201CB00012B/1802